Symphonies of the Heart

Symphonies of the Heart

Spiritual Harmony and the Quest for Holiness

By Greer G. Gordon

Pauline
BOOKS & MEDIA
Boston

The Scripture quotations contained herein are from the *New Revised Standard Version Bible,* copyright © 1989 by the Division of Christian Education of the National Council of the Churches of Christ in the U.S.A. Used by permission. All rights reserved.

ISBN 0-8198-7046-3

Copyright © 2001, Daughters of St. Paul

Printed and published in the U.S.A. by Pauline Books & Media, 50 Saint Pauls Avenue Boston, MA 02130-3491.

www.pauline.org

Pauline Books & Media is the publishing house of the Daughters of St. Paul, an international congregation of women religious serving the Church with the communications media.

1 2 3 4 5 6 7   07 06 05 04 03 02 01

Dedication

In memory of my mother,
Deasry Jackson Gordon,
and in gratitude for those
who have nurtured me in her absence:

Beverly Lartigue, C.S.J.,
Audrey Jones, O.S.B.,
and
Rita L. D. Wilkins

Contents

Introduction   ix

Part One: The Symphonic Source

Chapter One
    The Quest for the Holy   3

Chapter Two
    The Paths of Holiness   15

Part Two: The Movements of the Heart

Chapter Three
    The First Movement
    The Opening Theme: Wandering and
       Waiting   31

Chapter Four
    The Second Movement
    The Slowing Pace: Listening Hearts   45

Chapter Five
    The Third Movement
    The Struggling Heart: Dark Nights and
       Arid Days   57

Chapter Six
The Fourth Movement
The Inspiring Summit: God's Covenant
   of Love   73

Part Three: The Lived Reality

Chapter Seven
Spiritual Harmony: Balancing Work
   and Prayer   93

Chapter Eight
Spiritual Peace: Walking Justly
   and Acting Rightly   101

Introduction

The quest for God and the things of God is fundamental to the human person. The fact that we now stand at the threshold of a new millennium, the third Christian millennium, gives even greater impetus to humanity's spiritual quest. In anticipation of this new age, some are engaged in a variety of asceticisms that they hope will signal a return to the mystical path of jubilee. Others are engaged in practices of divination, which they regard as a means of foretelling the cataclysmic close of all time. Still others seek God either out of a true desire and joyful expectation or a trepidatious reluctance and fear of what the future might bring.

In our fragile humanity, we have come to find the unexpected and different frightening. Unfortunately, fear and reluctance are the most significant impediments to the modern search for the sacred. In an attempt to control what frightens us, some have latched onto outrageous theories and bogus doctrines—symptoms of the hope that God can be controlled or at least placated. Whether we are conscious of it or not, all of us are in pursuit of meaning. It is our hope that it will provide clarity and stability for our dreams, fears, and aspirations.

More than any other civilizations of the past, modern day marketplace-dwellers experience an anxiety of heart that leads to a plethora of empty pursuits. We feverishly engage in the pursuit of tangible goods or fleeting relationships that, once acquired, no longer hold our interest or give us delight. We spend the energy of our hearts in an endless quest for an indescribable something that we know will surpass anything we have ever known or imagined. We know that when we find it, our hearts will be able to arrive at a posture of fulfilled rest. But until that time, our hearts are filled with the deafening sound of our frenetic search.

Symphonies of the Heart: Spiritual Harmony and the Quest for Holiness is a reflection on the human person's desire for sanctification and the pursuit of holiness. It is about the quest for a relationship of hope in a world that has so many elements of despair. It is for those who have experienced a kind of wanderlust that has never found completion or satisfaction. It is intended for those who, like Augustine of Hippo, have known and experienced restlessness of heart.

A symphony is a magnificent musical composition designed by a gifted composer, performed by a large and diverse group of orchestral instrumentalists, under the leadership of a dynamic conductor. The symphony itself consists of several movements, in which both common themes and varied musical elements are woven together to produce the fullness of a musical masterpiece.

Such is God's presence in the human heart. The movements of God reflect life's harmonies and dissonances, life's simple and complex moments. God's movements transform our hearts, touching us so deeply that we experience them as symphonic orchestrations.

There are different ways to appreciate a musical symphony: as a professional musician, as an avid student and spectator, or as a novice who simply enjoys listening to good music. So, too, there are different ways to experience God's symphonies. Few are called to a contemplative religious life devoted exclusively to prayer and meditation. Many go through life avoiding what is explicitly religious, yet enjoying a lovely religious experience now and then. This book addresses those who find themselves somewhere between these two extremes: those of us who search for the Holy in our everyday lives, who need to learn how to listen and respond to the spiritual symphonies which God composes in our hearts, while continuing to be engaged fully in the busy world around us.

What most of us need is assistance in learning to pray where we are, in the marketplace. This is where God has called us and where God wants us to be; and that is good. Living in the here-and-now of the world is part and parcel of our baptismal call into relationship with God and with one another.

I sincerely believe that to be Christian means we are called to be people of prayer. If we are praying people, then we are not violent people; for violence goes against all that God is and calls us to be as people of faith. If there is one thing that truly is needed in our present world, it is the example of people who live and operate in the marketplace while being rooted in and guided by the ways and the things of God. We have only to remember what God said to Israel:

> You have seen what I did to the Egyptians, and how
> I bore you on eagles' wings and brought you to my-
> self. Now therefore, if you obey my voice and keep
> my covenant, you shall be my treasured possession
> out of all the peoples...you shall be for me a priestly
> kingdom and a holy nation... (Ex 19:4–6).

Knowing that we have been carried on wings of eagles, let us engage now in the pursuit of God and the things of God. Amen.

GREER G. GORDON
University of Massachusetts Dartmouth
September 8, 2000

Part One

The Symphonic Source

Chapter One
The Quest for the Holy

"From one ancestor [God] made all nations to inhabit the whole earth,…so that they would search for God and perhaps grope for him and find him…" (Acts 17:26–27).

As people of a technological age, we live in a society that is deeply afraid of the questions that await us in the stillness. The collective myth of our lives is that technology frees us to engage in the more meaningful dimensions of life. Yet, the fast-paced, high-stress orientation of modern society simply does not allow us to have enough time, in any given day, to do all the things that are requested by our families, friends, and work. No sooner do we respond to one set of demands than another set appears. In our hope to make the most of our lives, we schedule every second. Although we periodically take vacations, our leisure time is as frenetically oriented as our work time. As a result, we return from our vacations even more exhausted than before we left. Our lives are anything but self-reflective and still. We are constantly in motion.

Not only do we schedule our own lives, we also schedule the lives of our children, to make certain that they do not miss a single opportunity for enhancing their experience of childhood. Little wonder that children soon become teenagers who are ill equipped to handle the "boring" interludes of life's slower movements. Generation after generation, the pace quickens.

One of the greatest ironies of the current age is that our preoccupation with gathering information is accompanied by an avoidance of the quiet reflection necessary to give meaning to our collected data. In public and private we are besieged by people who either request or pass along information. From a simple machine in our homes, offices, or schools we can access libraries of information on nearly any subject imaginable. And what do we do with all this information? We store it in the expanded memories of our machines and continue our process of acquisition. However, without ever pausing to reflect upon the meaning of this data, the information we have gathered may have no frame of reference and may be meaningless to us.

Our high-tech age has simplified the process of knowledge acquisition, but it has created a nightmare for depth-level, integrated understanding. The most significant aspect of the acquisition of knowledge is the question that originally inspired the search. This is certainly the case in the quest for God and the things of God. Without the properly focused question, we can learn many things about God, but we will have absolutely no idea of how to relate to God or how to pursue a genuine relationship with God.

How do we begin our quest for God and the things of God? What questions may help us to recognize and experience the presence of the Composer of our hearts' symphonies? For many of us the search begins with a feeling of aloneness, or the unsettling thought that if indeed God does exist, it doesn't necessarily mean that God cares about our human concerns. This common human experience is described in a poignant scene in the stage play, "1776." In it, John Adams, standing dejected and alone, cries out: "Is anybody there? Does anybody care? Does anybody see what I see?" What John Adams expresses, while standing alone in a Philadelphia bell tower, is the profound sense of isolation that can overcome us in the midst of turmoil and uncertainty. During life's troubling moments, we may wonder if there really is a God. Does God see? Does God hear our cries? Does God know and understand our sorrow and desperation? Will God respond to our pleadings? It is frightening to think of a world with no God, or worse, a world with a God who does not care.

For many people, such questions about God are seen as bad or threatening. We would rather avoid the questions than risk the discovery that what we thought we knew might not be true. Perhaps we avoid asking questions out of a fear that this might be perceived as a sign that we have lost our faith. Still others, children of our humanistic, technological society, may feel embarrassed or put off by spiritual inquiry. Like Ellie Arroway in the movie, *Contact,* some dismiss religious questions as speculative and irrelevant because there is no possibility of empirical proof. It is unnerving to confront questions that science cannot answer.

The fact that we do not know all there is to know about God may leave us open to a level of fear that causes us to retreat from our quest for truth—which is ultimately God. The twentieth-century theologian, Paul Tillich, said that God is "Ultimate Concern" (cf. *Dynamics of Faith,* 1957, 10); the center of our deepest concerns and questions. If we do not actively seek God as the center of our concerns, we may miss the very opportunity God has placed before us to enter into a real relationship.

More often than not our questions and our doubts are the tools God uses to enable us to engage our intellectual powers and come to a better understanding of God and cre-

ation. Often, these questions arise in times of personal turmoil and suffering: the death of a loved one, serious illness,
financial hardship, or some other crisis that forces us to face
our human limitations. Suffering is never something to be
sought after or longed for; rather, suffering and distress are
simply part of our human reality. Pain, however, can provide
an opportunity for spiritual growth. Indeed, growth does
not happen without pain, and clear understanding is not
possible without some measure of questioning.

Most of us who have been raised in the Christian tradition
are afraid to admit there are times when we just are not really
sure that God is out there. If we are hesitant to admit our
questions about the power and presence of God, it's because
the very thought seems like a betrayal of God. We wonder
whether God is really the omniscient, omnipresent One we
were taught to expect God to be. Could our notions of
God—or even our belief in God at all—have been grounded
in error?

In this modern age when everything seems up for grabs, it
just doesn't seem reasonable to hold on to beliefs from ancient times. Listening to the wisdom of our elders and
assuming that their world is so far removed from our own,
we can think of their religious views as either irrelevant and
obsolete or incredibly, uniquely graced. Yet, perhaps the
sense of the "Ultimate Concern" has not changed all that
much over the ages. Indeed, had our ancestors in the faith
not asked difficult questions, then no one would have
sought, listened to, or passed on to us the manner in which
God has made, and continues to make, the Holy known
through human history. For "from one ancestor [God] made
all nations to inhabit the whole earth, ...so that they would
search for God and perhaps grope for him and find him—

though indeed he is not far from each one of us. For 'in him
we live and move and have our being'…" (Acts 17:26–28).

Obstacles to the Holy

The quest for the Holy is at once available to all and realized by relatively few. A number of obstacles may get in the
way of our spiritual growth and prove to be dead-ends rather
than pathways to God.

One of the first obstacles is the priority modern society
gives to immediate gratification. We want to see the results
of our efforts right away, and we seek the most expedient
method for achieving those results. We figure that all we have
to do is read the right books, sing the right songs and attend
the right church. We submit our minds and wills to would-
be charismatic personalities whom we trust to provide us
with the answers we need for instant spiritual success. We
give up our own freedom to wonder or to question, and
allow others to tell us what we ought to think or how we
ought to conduct our lives. This type of posture can easily
lead us astray, by substituting the ideals and practices of others for the slow, steady, and genuine growth of our own
relationship with God.

A second obstacle may be the fact that many people today
are afraid to ask questions of God or about God. Many of us
think that, as Christians, we should not even ask questions in
order to clarify what we profess to believe about God. However, if we do not allow ourselves to question, then the
relationship between faith (*what* we believe) and the quest
for God (the One *in whom* we believe) is lost.

Eventually this second obstacle leads some people to aban-
don the spiritual quest and to dismiss God as simply part of
the mythological and superstitious imaginings of the poorly

educated and unsophisticated. Those who respond in this way may become cynical regarding matters of faith, and reject all but rational perspectives on the incomprehensible complexities of life.

Others refrain from asking questions and instead embrace a simplistic belief system which inevitably crumbles in times of crisis. Such simplistic approaches present a number of obstacles in and of themselves. One is the danger of fundamentalism which, in effect, treats the Bible *not* as the living Word of God (contrary to fundamentalist claims), but rather as an idol, an object for memorization and literal interpretation. The mystery of God and the struggle to enter into a genuine relationship with the Holy are reduced to legalistic, irrefutable pat answers. Few who see the Bible from this point of view consider it the product of the spiritual turmoil and questioning of ancient peoples. Rather, it is God's words, which are easily comprehended by those who study them hard enough.

However, not all fundamentalism is scripturally based. Even more theologically oriented traditions can fall prey to fundamentalism. In such cases, Church teachings may be presented as rules governing the beliefs and behaviors of Church members with an unyielding exactness and absolute power. Jesus criticized a similar approach of the religious authorities in his community when he reminded them that the Sabbath is made for the people, not people for the Sabbath (cf. Mk 2:27). The danger of doctrinal or behavioral fundamentalism is that, like biblical fundamentalism, an externally imposed set of rules or beliefs is used as a litmus test for an individual's faith. Faced with significant personal, social, and political conflict, faithfulness may be judged according to standards of religious regulations rather than personal acts of conscience.

One final obstacle to the quest for the Holy is the problem of sin and guilt. There are individuals within the Christian community who teach that those who sin are no longer a part of the Church. According to the teachings of the Church, we are all sinners. This is why humanity is in need of salvation. Like the prodigal son of Luke 16, we are welcomed and forgiven by God. The Church, as the visible sign of Christ in the world, is called to be a reconciling presence and a beacon of hope for the sinner. Thus the idea that a person is outside of the Church because of sinfulness portrays an attitude of intolerance and judgment. This kind of misrepresentation of the teachings of the Church is the reason why many people leave the Church. Guilt-ridden and bitter, they assume that God, like some in the Church, has condemned them.

This reflects the confusion that exists between healthy and unhealthy guilt. Unhealthy guilt focuses one's attention on sin and leaves the sinner in a state of judgment and despair. But healthy guilt uses the occasion of sin as an opportunity for repentance. It doesn't focus on an individual's failure to be holy, but on God's promise to be gracious (cf. Ps 51). We cannot save ourselves; thus, we must turn to God for the healing grace that comes to us through repentance and reconciliation. We are not a Church of perfect people; rather, we are a community of prodigals called to seek and experience the forgiveness of a holy and loving God.

All of these obstacles to the quest for the Holy have a common source. Our fast-paced, fear-filled, quick-fix society lacks an adequate spiritual formation of its members, particularly within the Christian community. Adults with sophisticated technical training and secular savvy live spiritual lives at an adolescent level. They invest in simplistic and futile approaches to the spiritual, rather than in the depth-level struggle to enter into a relationship with the Holy. If we are to develop into spiritually mature believers, we must be willing to enter the struggle and ask the tough questions. Life is complicated, and quick fixes are inadequate for dealing with its challenges. Such is the design of the Creator, the Composer of our hearts' symphonies. We must learn to listen to the melodies and rhythms of the Holy, not through simplistic approaches and solutions but through the challenges, pain, and ordinariness of daily living.

Questions and the Quest

The freedom to ask difficult questions is what has allowed me to continue my quest for God. But those kinds of questions can only be answered with the passing of time and the persistence of prayer. Teresa of Avila said that the only thing anyone can teach us about prayer is how to start. God will teach us all else in time. I understand this to mean that God, at the appropriate moments in our lives, teaches us what we need to know in order to further develop the relationship we seek. Prayerful questioning—an openness to learn how to recognize God's presence and to embrace it—is an essential part of spiritual growth.

To question is a natural part of the human person. Whether it be an attempt to find hope in the midst of despair, or a means for seeking clarification, only by asking questions can we be led to the truth about God. It may be that in asking that seemingly desperate question: "Is anybody there?" we finally find God. The Scriptures provide us with countless examples of this. One figure who stands out as a paradigm of asking questions and thus finding God is Job.

The book of Job is the account of a good and upright person who, through his suffering and seeming abandonment by God, arrived at a moment when even he felt it was too much to handle. And in his questioning he cried out to God. As a result of his struggle with doubt and his questions addressed to God, Job found God in a way he had never known possible.

Job was a wealthy man, blessed with property, family, and well-being. Yet, in an instant everything was lost when Satan attempted to prove to God that Job's fidelity would last only as long as he prospered from God's favor. Job refused to curse God for his misfortune, and praised God instead, saying: "Shall we receive the good at the hand of God, and not receive the bad?" (Job 2:10a)

But soon even Job's self-esteem and character were called into question by his fellow believers. Three close friends offered Job neither insight nor comfort. They had nothing but platitudes and easy answers that reflected their simplistic view of faith. They automatically assumed that Job's suffering must have been due to some unacknowledged sin. If Job really had been faithful to God, they argued, then God would not have visited such evil upon him.

Because theirs was not a genuine knowledge of God, they relied on a religious formula that claimed that God always rewarded pious behavior with prosperity. Job's three friends were incapable of comprehending the profound questions and distress with which Job eventually confronted God. As Job painstakingly enumerated his many worthy acts and all the good he had done in his life, Job asked how God could give him over to such suffering. Job implied that he deserved better. In the midst of his outcry, the sky darkened and, as the clouds parted, God said to Job: "Where were you when I laid the foundation of the earth?" (Job 38:4)

Now, at a very young age my siblings and I learned that if we were unwise enough to show disrespect for our mother, we would soon rediscover our significance in the universe. Simply hearing her say: "To think, I carried you for nine months," would, without the slightest pause, reduce us to repentant little sinners desperately seeking both God's and Mother's forgiveness. This was her quiet way of reminding us that no matter how mature or accomplished we might someday become, we would never cease to be her children.

Just so, God reminded Job with that same kind of indisputable logic of one's true place. No matter how upright Job was, he was still a creature and God alone the Creator. Job found himself confronted with the infinite, the ineffable, the source of the universe and all that is. With that single question, God presented Job with the fact that human beings are incapable of fully comprehending God. Human beings, no matter how accomplished they may seem, will never cease to be creatures before God; we will never be equal to God.

Yet, God's response was not meant to further alienate Job, the creature, but simply and lovingly to enable him to enter into a deeper relationship with the Creator. The discipline of being reminded of his proper place in the universe affirmed Job's (as it did for my siblings and me) belief in the One who really does care for us.

Job sincerely repented of his arrogance toward God, but he also told God of how abandoned he had felt. This began a dialogue and genuine relationship between Job and God. Before this time of distress, Job's knowledge and worship of God were based only on what he had been taught by others. In a moment of insight, Job said to God: "I had heard of you by the hearing of the ear, but now my eye sees you; therefore I despise myself, and repent in dust and ashes" (Job 42:5–6). In the end, God restores Job's health and good fortune with more children and greater wealth than he had previously enjoyed—and he even lives to see the fourth generation of his heirs.

Job's questions brought him to a knowledge and an understanding of God that he had not known were possible. His distress and despair led him to question God; and, while God's response was perhaps not what Job expected, the result was greater than he could have asked for or imagined. Contrary to the popular view of easy solutions that his friends presented, Job struggled to engage in the process of developing a relationship with God. For the first time in his life, Job came to really know God. If Job had not asked his questions, he would not have come to a genuine relationship with God.

If we do not ask questions of God, then we will only know God through the experience of others and not through our own. Questions are a sign that we are actively seeking God. They are a sign of our desire to know the Creator and Composer of our hearts' symphonies, who is actively present within us and guiding us, like Job, in our journey toward spiritual harmony, wholeness, and peace. Through our questions we learn to recognize and experience the Holy and enter a dynamic relationship with our God.

· · · · · · · · · · ·

Is anybody there? Does anybody care? Does anybody see what I see? Hope!

"Hope in God; for I shall again praise him, my help and my God" (Ps 42:5b). Amen.

Chapter Two

The Paths of Holiness

"...The Spirit helps us in our weakness; for we do not know how to pray as we ought; but that very Spirit intercedes with sighs too deep for words" (Rom 8:26).

Our quest for God begins with questions, which are an acknowledgement of the fact that we are earnestly seeking the Holy. The next stage of this quest leads us into the development of a relationship with God. In and through our Baptism, we have been introduced into the life of God, but as adult believers we need to actively develop our relationship. The means by which we do this is prayer. Prayer is the vehicle for communication between God and the believer. But in order to understand how to pray, we will first consider the different types of prayer, and then discuss how one actually begins to pray.

Prayer: An Overview

Prayer within the Christian community can be divided into two categories: communal prayer or public worship, and individual or private prayer. The roles that these two categories of prayer play within the life of the believer are often confusing. In and through our public worship we gather with other believers to offer praise, supplication, and glory to God. We gain strength from public worship just by the fact that there are other people who believe in God and are seeking a relationship with God. In and through our private prayer we develop our own unique relationship with God. Frequently, when people speak about beginning to pray, this is the form of prayer they seek to understand. This chapter is designed as a response to that often expressed need. However, before addressing individual prayer, it is necessary to offer a few insights into the significance of communal prayer as well.

Most Christians gather for public worship once a week on Sunday, the day when, according to Christian tradition, the resurrection of the Lord Jesus Christ occurred. Thus, in the life of the Christian community, Sunday became the day for gathering publicly to profess belief in the One True God and to offer God praise and glory. Although Sunday worship is the most commonly practiced form of communal prayer, it is not the only type available within the Christian tradition. Communal or group prayer may take place at regularly scheduled gatherings of friends. For example, my aging aunt and several of her friends gather once a month to share lunch and to pray the rosary. They look forward to their time together and see it as a way to stay in touch in a prayerful way. During their gatherings they minister to one another's needs and place their cares and concerns before the Lord. It's an inspiring experience to be present in the midst of such faith. These women have found a way to fill their need to be present to God and one another in a manner that goes beyond formal Sunday worship and their regular phone calls or social visits. As Christian women, they recognize their need to establish a time to pray together in a way that is meaningful for their generation.

On the other hand, communal prayer can also be informal and spontaneous. A hospital patient and chaplain might join in prayer for healing. Family members might offer prayers of thanksgiving and blessing before a meal. Couples might pray together for God's guidance in significant life decisions or ordinary daily affairs. Put simply, any time two or more Christians gather in Christ's name, they are engaged in communal prayer.

Communal prayer is about believers coming together to support one another in their quest for God and the things of God. In it we support one another in our times of seeking God. Several years ago, I lived with a group of contemplative Benedictine women in their Saint Louis, Missouri monastery. The first day there my spiritual director ushered me up to an observation room at the top of the chapel. From that vantage, the entire, gigantic structure could be viewed. We looked down upon the one hundred choir stalls where the nuns gathered for public prayer, and she said to me: "There will be days when you will come here and cannot wait to engage in prayer and worship of God. But there will be other days when you will come into this holy place and find you would rather be anywhere other than here. On those days, we who are gathered here will carry and sustain you in your quest for God. By the same token, on the days when you are filled with a desire for God, you will carry someone who would rather be anywhere other than here." These words, spoken by a humble Benedictine nun, are for me the only real explanation of what it means to engage in communal prayer, and the relationship between prayer and the Church universal.

People who desire to learn more about individual or private prayer usually encounter four primary types. One type involves formula prayers such as the private recitation of the Lord's Prayer, the Rosary, the Serenity Prayer, or even the Psalms. A second type of private prayer is talking to God—

telling God about our trials and tribulations, or about our love for God. A third type of private prayer is reflecting upon God and the things of God. In this form of prayer we may use the Scriptures, or music, or a book that deals with matters of the spirit. We may even reflect upon the beauty around us, gazing upon a wondrous ocean or mountain scene, which heightens our awareness of the greatness of God's creation. A fourth type of private prayer is a listening in silence and stillness of heart, known as contemplation.

Contemplative prayer involves a process of emptying the mind and heart and, in that inner stillness, to be completely open to God's self-revelation. Rarely are lay people intentionally introduced to this form of prayer. However, some of us have been led into the experience of this contemplative prayer through the constant practice of one of the other forms of private prayer.

Several years ago my mother spoke of how she was always losing her place when praying the rosary. She would start out reciting the rosary and then suddenly find that she could not remember where she was in her prayer. Thinking she was forgetful, she would simply start over from the beginning. Although my mother may indeed have been forgetful, it seems more likely that, in the constant repetition of the rosary, she had emptied her heart and mind and had been brought into contemplation by God.

Contemplation is the result of an individual's sincere commitment to the practice of prayer. There are several techniques that may facilitate a believer's entering into this form of prayer, and I will treat them later. However, it is a type of prayer that requires perseverance and patience, for it means that we are committed to waiting on God. Those who are just beginning prayer may find it easier to start with one or more of the other types of prayer before attempting to move into contemplative forms of prayer.

Starting the Practice of Prayer

Prayer is communication with God through which we engage in and maintain a personal relationship with the Holy. As with all relationships, a relationship with God must be valued and cultivated. Five initial steps are necessary for beginning this communication with the Divine: recognition, stillness, reflection, time, and a path.

- First, we must recognize that communication with God is not optional to our Christian commitment. Prayer is essential to the fabric of our lives as believers.

- The second step is the ability to be still. We have to be able to put aside our compulsion for frenetic activity.

- Third, we must assume an attitude of reflection. To put it simply, we must enable ourselves to think deeply.

- The fourth step is a willingness to make time to be present before God. We control time; time does not control us. We will find time for prayer if we decide it is a value we want to pursue in our lives.

- The fifth and final step in beginning prayer is discovering a path of prayer that fits us. Each of us is a unique person and our relationship with God is also unique; thus, we must find a style of communication that is best suited to our personalities.

Recognizing a Necessary Relationship

In order to begin prayer, the adult believer must recognize that we come to know and accept God for ourselves only by means of a direct communication with God. Through prayer

we actively participate in the development of a love relationship with the Holy. For any number of reasons, the average
believer has placed such an emphasis on the public prayer of
the Church that the necessity of private prayer has been lost.
Many of us have come to regard private communication with
God as optional, and as such, private prayer has become
something we do only when we are in need.

However, our private communication with God, individual prayer, is an essential element of adult faith. Without
it we have no relationship with God. Without it we praise
and worship God out of a sense of obligation, or on the basis
of hearsay, or out of a fearful sense of damnation. In any
case, private prayer is often not practiced out of a desire to
come to know the One who lovingly created, saved, and
continues to guide us. Thus, we need to decide that we want
to know God, and to do whatever it takes to achieve this.

As believers, we must also be willing to admit that a relationship with God is important to us. This admission
encourages a willingness to take the risk of opening ourselves
to God. As we reflect upon the importance of our relationship with God, it may be helpful to consider some of the
other meaningful relationships in our lives. If we pause for a
moment and think about someone we really love—a spouse,
a family member, or a dear friend—we can reflect on how we
came to love that person. Did we just instinctively love these
people? I doubt it. The people we love are those individuals
we have risked letting inside ourselves. We have allowed
them to see our goodness and kindness, but also our faults
and flaws. In other words, they are the people we have allowed to really know us, people with whom we have spent
and wasted time. Why do we think our relationship with
God will be any different? We are human beings, and the
way we come to love others is by getting to know them and

by allowing them to get to know us. So, too, we must be willing to discover God in the silence of the love relationship that is prayer.

Developing a Posture of Stillness

Stillness is usually a posture that adults hope their very active children will assume. But we rarely realize how little time we actually spend being still. Our society finds rapid movement essential for a productive existence; yet, we would probably accomplish more if we were more rested or did things out of a posture of stillness. Stillness is a posture of the heart. It is an attitude or a mindset, a way of moving through life without being perturbed or distressed. From this posture of centeredness we can approach all of life, and especially God. We must be like the prophet Elijah who discovered that God was not in the fierce wind or the earthquake, but in the stillness and silence that followed the storm (cf. 1 Kgs 19:11–13). Stillness is the posture of rest, and in prayer we rest in God. Thus, it is essential that we cultivate within our hearts a posture of stillness, a posture of peace.

Assuming an Attitude of Reflection

One of the factors that distinguish human beings from other forms of animal life is our ability to be consciously reflective and, in particular, self-reflective. Reflection is a process of intentional thought; we actually decide to reflect upon something. However, it is a practice that we can subconsciously put aside. We can actually fall out of the practice of reflection. The busier we become, the greater the likelihood that we will no longer engage in the active process of reflection with any frequency. Yet, it is a most relaxing process that also helps us in our ability to see the choices we have before us with greater clarity.

Training in reflection can begin quite early in life. Without realizing it, my parents greatly contributed to my practice of reflection. Whenever I was in trouble they would say: "You need to reflect on what you've done," or, "Go and contemplate what you've done." The 1950s precursor of the "time-out" movement formed many active children into reflective adults.

To engage in prayer we must exercise our ability to reflect. We must be willing to be alone with ourselves and our own thoughts. If we are not comfortable being within ourselves, then we will not be comfortable with God's presence within us. If the truth about ourselves makes us uncomfortable, then we will certainly be uncomfortable with the truth of God. We must cultivate the practice of being alone with the truth of ourselves and be willing to assess our lives. And the only way to do this is to pause daily and think about how we have conducted ourselves. This daily practice brings us to that deeper way of being human which is the process of being self-reflective. Self-reflection allows us to move more easily to a posture of reflection upon the Scriptures and God's presence in the ordinary realities of our lives.

Making Time for Prayer

Prayer is something that we can do at any time and any place—even in a crowd. It involves the process of withdrawing into ourselves and reflecting upon our relationship with God. We have to carve out the space and time to engage in prayer, because it does not simply happen. Thus, it is necessary to be in touch with our own movements and dynamics.

If we are too filled with the roar of life, then soft music may help us to settle down into a posture of stillness. I particularly like classical music. To spend some time listening to a little music and reading allows us to simply relax. Wondrous music brings us more deeply in touch with the music of God and opens us to the movements within. The use of music in prayer can be a prelude to our discovery of God's symphonies within our hearts.

I am one of those people who likes to work very late into the night. I love the silence and stillness of the night. Thus, I have learned that the best time for me to pray is in the midst of night's stillness, especially in the winter. As Robert Frost knew well, there is nothing quite like the stillness of a snowy New England evening to inspire an awe-filled reflection on the meaning of life.

In beginning your schedule of daily prayer, you may have to figure out which hours of the day you feel least concerned about life's demands and distractions. What are the times least taken up with family or business matters? What is the best time for you to look inside yourself and begin to focus on the Lord? Choose a time when you are least likely to be disturbed or interrupted by anyone or anything. I know people who pray in the morning at their kitchen tables, or on a morning walk, or while gardening. Pick the time and setting best for you.

Many of us may look at those in religious life and believe that to be a person of prayer, we should spend as much time in prayer as they do. But some of us can't even deal with the thought of an hour of prayer time. Don't be too concerned with the amount of time you take; be more concerned about the quality of the time. I find that fifteen minutes is a relatively comfortable segment for most busy people starting to pray regularly. Usually people are able to find this amount of time in their schedules. If we can't find fifteen minutes out of the 1,440 minutes in a day, then we probably should take a radical look at the level of activity we have allowed into our lives. In any case, we will make certain that we have time for prayer if the significant issue for us is improving the quality of our relationship with God. And when we do make time with consistency, the finer points will be worked out as God leads us along the path of prayer.

Discovering a Path of Prayer

Once we've established the best time for prayer, we can begin to discover what type of prayer fits us best. The effort to discover a path of prayer that suits our personalities is essential, because it will help us to form the habit of prayer. Sometimes, however, looking at how we feel drawn to pray may be difficult, for it forces us to examine the nature of our own developing relationship with God.

Some people need to be more emotive, more expressive, in their way of praying. Rather than being quietly seated and still, some need an activity to aid them in prayer. Playing a musical instrument, singing, using gestures or dance are other creative ways to engage our passionate hearts and emotive souls in communicating with God.

Other people may struggle with their own wills and with letting go of their own agendas so that God may lead them. In these cases, when we have no words or are too filled with our own words, we may find it helpful to begin prayer by reading from the abundant sources available in the Scriptures or from some spiritual writings. I am partial to the writings of Saint Teresa of Avila. I have found that this type of reading as a prelude to prayer assists me in keeping focused and centered on God and allows my own will to gradually give way to God's.

Some people like to use very clear, concrete images for prayer. These individuals may find reflecting upon biblical stories a very good approach. I am particularly drawn to the stories within the Gospel according to Luke. Luke's clear images and details make it possible not only to picture the scene, but also to imagine oneself within it. This praying with the Scriptures is an excellent way to allow the Word of God to speak to us in prayer. We can use any of the Gospel accounts or passages from any one of the books of the Bible. We may select a passage, read it very slowly, and then allow it to wash over us. We may even want to repeat over and over a verse or phrase that strikes our hearts deeply. This allows the Word to inform and influence our thoughts and the content of our lives. The Bible then is not just a book or a source for nice quotations, but part of the fabric of our being. This is how the Word of the Lord comes to be ever in our hearts and on our lips.

For those who are less inclined toward concrete ways of prayer, and find that images distract rather than assist them in their pursuit of God, there are other paths. If someone feels drawn toward a kind of emptiness of thought or consciousness before the presence of God, the best approach to prayer may be a Christian *mantra;* that is, the repetitious recitation of a word, a phrase, a brief prayer, or a scriptural verse. The process of repeating a prayer over and over again begins to empty the mind and open the heart to the movements of God. As I already mentioned, my mother felt very concerned over losing her place in the rosary. When I suggested that she should simply continue her rosary, it was because I realized that her constant repetition of the "Hail Mary" was functioning as a mantra. Through this repetition, her heart was being emptied of the sense of her own presence and opened to the presence of God.

There are a number of examples of the use of a Christian mantra as a path of prayer. Early Christians used the Jesus Prayer: "Lord Jesus Christ, Son of the living God, have mercy on me, a sinner." The late Dom John Main, a noted

Benedictine monk of Ealing Abbey, suggested praying the
early Christian prayer *"Maranatha"* (Come, Lord). Those
who are inclined toward this form of prayer may find speaking with those who have practiced it, or reading some of the
extensive works on the subject, very helpful.

There is a wonderful story from the early centuries of the
Church about a desert monk who practiced this form of contemplative prayer. According to the story, this elderly monk
had spent the majority of his life in the desert regions of Asia
Minor engaged in prayer. One day a young man, new to the
monastic life, engaged the older monk in a conversation
about prayer. He said: "Abba (Father), can you tell me how
you pray?" The elder monk responded gently: "I set aside a
time, I sit, and I become present to the Lord." The younger
monk, said: "Yes, that is wonderful. But *what* do you pray?"
In a somewhat matter-of-fact manner, the elder monk responded: "Our Father."

Encouraged by the possibility of receiving concrete direction on how to proceed in prayer, the younger monk replied:
"The 'Our Father.' That is a good prayer. But pardon me if I
ask, how far do you get in the 'Our Father'?" In an even
gentler tone than before, the elderly monk simply said: "Our
Father." The younger monk, thinking that his elder might
not have heard his question clearly, rephrased it: "Yes, Abba,
but as you pray the 'Our Father,' how much of the prayer do
you say?" With a look of heartfelt compassion, the elder
monk responded, "Our Father."

What the elder monk was trying to tell the young monk
was that he had prayed the "Our Father" in silence and in
peace for so many years, it had entered into the depths of his
being. Thus, in the latter years of his life, the loving utter-
ance of the words, "Our Father," was enough to bring him

into God's presence. This is prayer of the heart. And out of such prayer flow the symphonies of the heart.

The most important part of beginning to pray is the willingness to engage and be engaged by God. Beginning to pray seems difficult, perhaps even overwhelming. However, we simply need to keep before us the fact that we have:

- a need for God's presence;

- the ability to develop a posture of stillness;

- the capacity to be reflective;

- a need to take the time to be with God;

- and, within the tradition of the Church,
  a variety of prayer paths that can lead us to God.

. . . .

Finally, when we are unable to remember any of these points, we can simply recall with Saint Paul that we are never alone. When we are at a loss for words, God's Spirit pleads for us with prayers beyond all words (cf. Rom 8:26). Thus may we learn to be attentive to God's symphonies within us. Amen.

Part Two

The Movements of the Heart

Chapter Three

The First Movement
The Opening Theme:
Wandering and Waiting

*"Those who wait for the Lord shall renew their strength,
they shall mount up with wings like eagles..." (Is 40:31).*

In the opening movement of a musical symphony, the conductor establishes the atmosphere and character of the symphony. The major themes, rhythms, and mood introduced in the first movement fill the listener with a sense of anticipation, a feeling that the best is still to be realized as the symphony unfolds.

In the symphony of the heart, the opening theme often reflects two motifs: wandering and waiting. The wandering motif describes the first steps some individuals experience in getting to know the fullness of God's presence. Others begin their spiritual journey with delighted anticipation as they wait on the Lord. These contrasting motifs of wandering and waiting are present in everyone's spiritual quest. Most believers, however, tend to have a stronger initial experience of one or the other. Thus, an awareness of the characteristics of each motif helps us not only to recognize but also to appreciate how they are reflected in the early moments of our spiritual quest.

The Motif of Wandering

Everyone, even the most focused person, wanders at some point. And at one time or another everyone lives the agony of waiting. Wandering is usually associated with the young, and waiting with either the extremely young or extremely old—those who are unable to demand their right not to have to wait. We try to teach the young patience, and we expect the elderly to be their mentors. As for those who are in their so-called "productive years," we expect that they neither wander nor wait.

This phenomenon reflects the spiritual problem that plagues modern society. We are compelled to search for God and the things of God, and not to wander may inhibit a person from taking the initial steps of that quest. Likewise, a lack of willingness to wait may mean that we as creatures have forgotten that we are always at the avail of our Creator. We wait on God. There is a French word, *disponible,* that describes something as being at the disposal of, or available to, something else. It is in this sense that the human being is at the disposal of the Creator. In relation to God, we are *disponible.* Our inability to wait or to be available to God often translates into our being too busy to recognize God in our midst. Because we have lost a proper understanding of the significance of both wandering and waiting, we cannot enter into the proper attitude for igniting or reigniting the flame of our relationship with the Holy.

People today tend to think that all wandering is indicative of an unproductive and underdeveloped mind. However, the people of the mid-fifth century C.E. recognized wandering as a sign of the great battle between God's will and the individual's. Times of wandering, confusion, or ambivalence can actually be the most significant periods in life leading to change. Augustine of Hippo is a classic example of how God can lead a person from the motif of wandering to a posture of listening. In his *Confessions,* Saint Augustine described his own notorious period of wandering as restlessness of heart: "My heart is restless, O Lord, until it rests in you" *(Confessions,* VIII:21). Restlessness of heart often grows into a passionate desire for God that develops into a listening heart. When the wanderer's passionate, undirected quest is transformed into a focused, single-mindedness, no thing and no one can take God's place. Then restless wandering becomes a posture in which listening is the most valuable of human qualities. The heart singularly focused on God is the heart that is intent upon knowing God and all that God wants for that soul.

In many respects, Augustine's example of wandering mirrors the type of wandering that many people in our society experience today. Intelligent, well educated, economically comfortable, Augustine could find no meaning or challenge in what the established world of academia or religion had to say. He put his energies into the pursuit of matters of the mind, with the hope that he might discover an ideology that would provide some sense of meaning and intellectual challenge. He knew he needed something, but he didn't know what; so he pursued many things that ultimately failed to provide meaning or truth.

For years, Augustine followed a number of paths that never really brought him a sense of fulfillment. Eventually, his mother, Saint Monica, convinced him to meet one of the well-known leaders of the Christian community: Ambrose, the Bishop of Milan.

In his spiritual autobiography, *Confessions,* Augustine describes how Ambrose deeply impressed him from the first moment they met. Augustine found Ambrose to be a gifted intellectual who not only had a desire for the truth, but who also seemed to have a profound sense of the truth. Through Ambrose, Augustine's wandering heart found rest in God, whom he had come to know from his own personal experience.

In the Scriptures we discover that the process of wandering is intimately intertwined with the necessity of waiting. Wandering is often the catalyst God uses to bring Israel to a posture of waiting. The Israelites did not come to know God for themselves until after their time of wandering in the desert. In the book of Numbers we are told that the ancient Israelites grew impatient with God's process of forming them into a people. They were tired of wandering and began to complain, lamenting that they had been better off in Egypt (cf. Num 14:1–3). Yet, when God brought the Israelites to the entrance of the Promised Land, they complained again. This time they were afraid of the people already living there.

Because of their faithlessness, and in order to form the next generation in faith, God decided that the Israelites would remain in the desert. They would get to know God better as they wandered, learning what it meant to be God's people. God said to them:

> …I have heard the complaints of the Israelites, which they complain against me…. Not one of you shall come into the land in which I swore to settle you, except Caleb son of Jephunneh and Joshua son of Nun. But your little ones…I will bring in, and they shall know the land that you have despised. But as for you, your dead bodies shall fall in the wilderness. And your children shall be shepherds in the wilderness for forty years, and shall suffer for your faithlessness, until the last of your dead bodies lies in the wilderness. According to the number of the days in which you spied out the land, forty days, for every

day a year, you shall bear your iniquity, forty years, and you shall know my displeasure. I the Lord have spoken... (Num 14:27b, 30–35a).

The ancient Israelites could not tolerate a climate of waiting. They did not yet have a sufficient knowledge or relationship with God to accept or enter into a waiting posture. They needed a much more active stance: the illusion of seeking God. It was an illusion because God had already found them, and even delivered and protected them. But they could not yet accept that posture. They needed to feel that *they* had looked for and found God themselves; their wandering and waiting were a necessary part of that process.

The people of Israel needed time to grow and develop a sense of themselves and a sense of God. Their forty years of wandering and waiting in the wilderness was just what they needed to learn how to live as God's people. In time the Israelites would formulate prayers to recall their quest for God: "O God, you are my God, I seek you, my soul thirsts for you; my flesh faints for you, as in a dry and weary land where there is no water" (Ps 63:1).

One of my sacred recollections of my mother was the first time I learned that I could be in public outside her gaze or sight. In the late summer of 1957, my mother and I went into downtown Baton Rouge to buy my very first parochial school uniform. I tried on the skirt with the required first-grader suspenders (all the time Mother assuring me that one day I would have enough hips to be able to wear a skirt without the aid of suspenders!). Then we moved over to what appeared to be, from the perspective of a tiny five-year-old, huge, cube-shaped tables with two very deep drawers. The tables were so big I couldn't see over them even when I stood on tiptoe.

Mother stood at the table, searching through package after package for a size 6x blouse—that way I would have
plenty of room to grow during the next school year. I did
not much care for shopping, and by the time we began that
blouse hunt, I had pretty much determined that it was time
to move on to the fresh popcorn treat Mother had promised. Restless and uncomfortable with waiting, I started
walking around the table. Engulfed in my own five-year-old
fantasies, I did not realize that I had moved several times
around the table until I had "lost" my mother. I suddenly
became conscious of the fact that I could neither see nor
hear her. I ran around corner after corner of the cube-shaped
tables, thinking that she was right there; but she wasn't.

Trying not to panic, I continued looking for Mother until
I finally caught a glimpse of her polka-dot skirt. In a pan-
icked tone that can only come from a small, frantic child, I
cried out and ran to her in tears, telling her how I thought I
had lost her and how glad I was that I had finally found her.
Then she spoke words in the soft Baton Rouge drawl that
was almost uniquely hers, and that still to this day give me
comfort: "Oh, Greer, Mother's right here. I had you in my
gaze all the time. I always had my eye on you." I thought
that I needed to find her, but she had found me before I had
even needed to look. She had never lost me. I, on the other
hand, needed to wander in order to learn that I needed to
seek after her. Only five years old, I could not yet stand patiently and wait.

When we are not yet able to wait, wandering becomes a
significant transition to our posture of waiting. We need to
run around for awhile, to look here and there and seemingly
everywhere, only to return to where we started. Those who
wander in their spiritual quest tend not to assume that other
people's experience of God will necessarily be their own. Like

the Israelites in the wilderness, this new generation of seekers may discover through their search for God that the truth of God is already in their midst. But it will only be discovered when they learn to wait on God.

Wandering is not, in and of itself, a negative thing; it can provide the contrast and challenge needed to recognize and appreciate God's presence. Like Augustine, one may come to recognize the absence of the peace of God in the restlessness and confusion of a life without God. Like the Israelites, one may come to grow gradually, through trial and error, into a relationship with God and an understanding of living as a member of God's people. Finally, like a small child in a big world, sometimes we need the wandering that is precipitated by waiting; we need to experience the frightening loss of God in order to really understand that God is faithful and never loses us.

The Motif of Waiting

The movement toward the Holy begins for some with the restless activity of wandering and develops gradually into the posture of waiting. As with wandering, so too waiting is an element of the heart's symphonic development. However, for most of us waiting is very difficult and uncomfortable. Waiting, in modern day parlance, means someone has power or control over us and our time. As a result, we tend to think of waiting as simply a matter of wasting time, which requires extraordinary patience. But there are positive ways in which waiting can enrich our early and ongoing relationship with God. Waiting can be active or passive. It can be seen as a time of preparation and readiness, or of abandonment and peace. Those who approach their spiritual journey in a posture of waiting discover that it is a time of hope and anticipation that requires patience and discipline.

Barriers to Waiting

The twentieth century has witnessed a growing sense of urgency to maximize productivity and success. In no area of human activity is this more apparent than in communication. Just a century ago, society hailed the telegraph and telephone as major breakthroughs in speeding messages between parties over long distances. Today, we send overnight mail, faxes, voice mail, and electronic mail. Each of these vehicles of communication promises to cut the time needed for the transmission of instantaneous questions that expect instantaneous responses. Anyone who feels satisfied with slow communication such as the ordinary postal service is looked on with disdain.

If this is the case with regard to simple communication between human beings, it's little wonder that communication with God is viewed with even greater skepticism. To assume a posture of waiting for God to speak to our hearts can seem like sheer absurdity. For those who are uncertain of God's existence, the logical conclusion is that waiting for an uncertainty is a waste of time. Even the most stalwart believers may be uncomfortable with waiting for God to act in God's own time and on God's own terms. These individuals may try to "jump start" God's communication with them, rather than wait until they are ready to hear God clearly.

Two barriers to waiting, skepticism and impatience, are reflected in two stories, one from the arts and the other from Scripture. In Samuel Becket's play, *Waiting for Godot,* two figures are portrayed waiting, infinitely waiting, for the arrival of a mysterious individual identified only as Mr. Godot. In the course of the play, the audience slowly comes to the realization that the characters are locked in an infinite cycle of repetitive acts which reflect the fact that their longed-for guest, who represents God, will never arrive. What unfolds is a psychological analysis of the impact of indefinite waiting upon an individual. Two characters, alone on a partially lit stage, stand vigilantly watching the passersby. Periodically, one asks in vain of the other if a passerby is Mr. Godot. Dejected, the two protagonists step away and continue to wait for the one who never comes.

The two main characters in Becket's play are waiting for life to come back to them. All of their existence is about waiting; but their waiting belies a sense of skepticism, hopelessness, and despair. The godlike figure of Mr. Godot does not come because the protagonists are in hell. Hell is waiting without hope of fulfillment, without ever hearing or ever knowing if God is coming. The play dramatically portrays a common fear in modern society: God is not coming, and therefore, waiting for God is pointless. For the modern spiritual seeker, this kind of skepticism and hopelessness creates its own hellish experience.

A second story appears in 1 Samuel 13. It is about Saul, the first king of Israel. Early in Saul's reign, while he is still trying to learn how to serve God as king of God's people, Saul becomes impatient and makes a mistake that costs him dearly. Saul is about to go to war, but is instructed to wait seven days for the prophet Samuel to arrive and offer a blessing to God for success in battle. When Samuel does not arrive on time, and Saul's people begin to lose hope and become restless, Saul decides to offer the sacrifice himself. He gives in to his impatience and fear instead of trusting that Samuel will come as promised. Immediately after Saul offers the sacrifice, Samuel appears. Not only does he chastise Saul for his rash judgement, but he also warns the king that such actions jeopardize his reign.

All of us have had the experience of waiting for something delayed, of not knowing if a person or event will eventually come about, or if the planned encounter will be cancelled altogether. This can be disconcerting and unsettling. Throughout the ages, however, God has spoken to people's hearts in time, if only they wait in patience and hope. The stories of Mr. Godot and King Saul demonstrate the dangers of the alternative. Yielding to impatience and skepticism can impede the development of God's symphonies within our hearts, for patience and trust are foundational themes of God's music. If our first step toward God is one of trust, despite the uncertainty of knowing how the symphony will sound, then we can learn to wait patiently for God to speak to our hearts.

Benefits of Waiting

As believers, we don't know exactly how or when God's symphony will resound in our hearts. Certainly, at the earliest stages of our journey, it may be difficult even to recognize God's voice. But the path to enter into a relationship with God involves patience, taking one slow, simple, steady step at a time toward spiritual growth.

The trick to waiting is to maintain a spirit of patient trust in, and joyful anticipation of, the God whom we desire. Admittedly, this is more easily said than done, especially when we wait for someone we don't see. But, unlike the characters in Becket's play, we don't have to wait in hellish hopelessness. Quite the contrary, this is the beginning of an exciting new journey, so our waiting can be full of joy.

In the Gospel of Luke, the story of Mary and Elizabeth serves as a good example of a hope-filled waiting in the first movement of God's symphony of the heart. There is no metaphor more appropriate for this experience than a pregnant woman eagerly anticipating the birth of her first child. According to this Gospel account, Mary, who is pregnant with Jesus, visits her older relative Elizabeth, who is pregnant with John the Baptist. Both women are experiencing the common anxiety of expectant mothers, but added to this is the stress of finding themselves pregnant under unusual circumstances. Yet, even the babies *in utero* respond with joy to their meeting. Both mothers, without fully knowing what lies ahead, nonetheless trust God's promises—so much so, that Elizabeth proclaims Mary blessed for believing "...that there would be a fulfillment of what was spoken to her by the Lord" (Lk 1:45).

As an introductory motif in the heart's symphony, waiting can be a lot like expecting the birth of a baby. Pregnancy is a time of anxious anticipation: uncertainty over what the unborn child will be like, what promises and challenges the birth will bring. An expectant mother can be happy, frightened, anxious, and hesitant all at the same time. The pregnancy gives the parents (and, in fact, the family and friends as well) time to adjust in order to accommodate this new life and prepare for the changes a child will bring.

The spiritual seeker also needs time to adjust to the fact that God is initiating a relationship which will enable him or her to experience the world in a whole new way. Perhaps one's symphony will begin with a growing awareness of and sensitivity to God's majesty revealed through the beauty of creation. Prayerful reflection on the psalms may help guide one's thoughts and focus one's ability to hear God's first strains of music in one's heart. A number of psalms reflect this theme, including Psalms 8, 104, and 139. Each of these prayer-hymns demonstrates how spiritual seekers from ancient times first came to know God through the majesty of creation. Those ancient reflections can speak as powerfully to the modern heart waiting on the Lord as they did to generations before.

Not everyone's first movement of waiting involves such joyful wonder. This can also be a painful time (again, not unlike some experiences of pregnancy). The pain may reflect a change in lifestyle that one must undergo in order to become receptive to God's presence. Waiting for the Holy may make the seeker aware of how he or she has been alienated from self, from others, and from God. What do we do when we find ourselves in a situation of sin? Waiting provides an opportunity for God to heal us, to enter our lives and transform us. Not knowing what our new life with God will be like can seem scary. But, as Saint Paul reminds us, we hope in precisely what we do not yet see—a life of holiness which we must await with patience (cf. Rom 8:24–25). God will help us to gradually change so that our lives will reflect the harmony and peace that only God can give.

What about the problem of impatience? How can we avoid rushing God rather than trusting God to act in God's own time? It helps to keep in mind that the very process of waiting is an opportunity for growth and learning. Rather than focusing on the goal—wanting to know God, to experience spiritual peace, etc.—one can actively engage the waiting process by preparing for God's movement in one's life.

Jesus tells a parable which illustrates nicely this posture of active waiting. Matthew 25 opens with the parable about ten bridesmaids who are preparing for a wedding banquet. The bridegroom is delayed, much like Mr. Godot in Becket's play. However, five of the bridesmaids take advantage of the extended waiting period by buying more oil for their lamps. When the bridegroom finally arrives, the other five, who had been impatient and unfocused, are left behind because their lamps have burned out, while the wise ones are ready and welcomed.

Our own experience of waiting with patience and hope can be like this. Rather than focusing on the future, we should center on the present moment. If we reflect on the changes that need to take place in our lives in order to hear God's symphony in our hearts, then we will indeed be filled with hope and joy as this first movement begins.

This chapter began with a discussion of the French word *disponible,* and it seems appropriate to conclude on the same note. Whether the opening motif of a heart's symphony is characterized more by wandering or by waiting, the hope is that early on, the seeker will develop a posture of "disposability"—to be open to however God guides one's spiritual journey. To be at another's disposal has almost negative connotations in English, suggesting that a person is expendable and to be "disposed of." Actually, *disponible* means the exact opposite, because it implies potential and promise. To be at God's disposal means that, like Augustine of Hippo, or Mary and Elizabeth, everything has been put in order, arranged, and prepared so that our new life with God may begin.

. . . .

The first movement toward the Holy must involve openness. Whether the seeker is a wanderer or waiter, the first step is one of promise and hope of fulfillment. Like a musical interlude, these initial motifs introduce powerful themes that will be developed later. For the Lord "does not faint or grow weary.... He gives power to the faint, and strengthens the powerless. Even youths will faint and be weary, and the young will fall exhausted; but those who wait for the Lord shall renew their strength, they shall mount up with wings like eagles, they shall run and not be weary, they shall walk and not faint" (Is 40:28–31). Amen!

Chapter Four

The Second Movement
The Slowing Pace: Listening Hearts

> *"...Blessed are your eyes, for they see, and your ears, for they hear. Truly I tell you, many prophets and righteous people longed to see what you see, but did not see it, and to hear what you hear, but did not hear it" (Mt 13:16–17).*

Sometimes people hear symphonies without ever actually listening to them. Likewise, with God's symphonies in our hearts, we may hear God's voice in the midst of all the noise and distraction around us, but never realize the message God is trying to convey. We must develop opportunities to give an open and listening heart to God, and to get to know God's voice in our daily routine.

As an undergraduate in college, I remember one particularly bad day. My mother was ill and I had just received a phone call that her condition had worsened. Then, when I went to check my mail, I found a letter from a friend back home informing me of the death of one of our high school friends. While I stood there in shock, the dean of students passed by. She knew me because I was a resident assistant in one of the dormitories. As she drew near, she must have seen the look on my face because she asked if anything was wrong.

I replied, "Yes, I just received news of the death of one of my friends." As soon as I completed my statement, she said, "Well, I hope you have a really good day." Then she walked away, and I just stood there stunned. I realized that she really had not heard what I had said to her. She was a caring person who was known for her good communication with the students. But on that day, the communication was strictly one-way, and not at all effective.

For most of us, communication with God is like my experience with that dean. God speaks to us, but we just don't hear what is being said. We don't listen; thus, we do not hear God. How can we know what God is saying to us? How can we tune in to the voice of God?

Hearing, Listening and Understanding

When God first called Isaiah, the prophet heard a confusing message:

> [The Lord] said, "Go and say to this people:
> 'Keep listening, but do not comprehend; keep
> looking, but do not understand.'
>
> Make the mind of this people dull, and stop their
> ears, and shut their eyes, so that they may not look
> with their eyes, and listen with their ears, and
> comprehend with their minds, and turn and be
> healed" (Is 6:9–10).

Isaiah had strong faith in God, and he saw evidence of God's promises and God's presence all around him. Those to whom he preached, however, heard him with closed hearts. Even the kings who asked for Isaiah's advice would not abide by his message. They did not understand that, since Isaiah was listening closely to God, his words were trustworthy. They did not want to make the effort to listen to God closely, as Isaiah had, in order to discern what God was saying to them.

Recently a friend related to me her and her husband's distress over visits from another couple who were her dear friends. Both couples were near retirement. The two women had been college friends and had gotten together periodically over the years. My friend confessed to me, "You know, I enjoy Margaret's visits so much. Margaret and I went to college together and so obviously spend a lot of time catching up on news when she comes once or twice a year. But our husbands wind up talking together, and the problem is that Margaret's husband talks all the time! My husband rarely gets a word in, and he becomes really tired of having to do all the listening. He keeps saying to me, 'That fellow goes on and on. I don't think he even breathes!' These visits are really hard on my husband."

My friend's husband felt distressed over having to spend time listening to someone who talked too much, and perhaps what was said may not have been particularly interesting, edifying, or life-giving for him. However, listening to God is different. Although it takes a while to recognize God's voice, once we hear it and learn to listen intently, we will come to gradually understand the messages God places in our hearts.

Recognizing God's Voice

Several of the great biblical prophets—Isaiah, Samuel, and Moses, to name a few—heard God's voice clearly calling them. For example, Samuel was a young boy serving in the temple at Shiloh. Awakened from his sleep one night, God called Samuel three times before he recognized that the voice was God's (cf. 1 Sm 3). Likewise, Moses heard God's voice clearly on the mountain of Horeb, but struggled to comprehend just who that God was whose voice bellowed forth from the burning bush (cf. Ex 3).

One day a student complained that it seems much harder to hear and recognize God's voice today than in biblical times. "God doesn't just talk to people anymore, like you read about in the Bible," she insisted. "How are we supposed to hear God speaking?" I am not so sure the problem is that God speaks differently today than in times past; rather, we haven't learned to discern God's voice or take the time to listen to what God has to say.

In Plato's *Republic,* there appears a well-known text called "The Myth of the Cave." This story describes a group of individuals who have been incarcerated in a cave for so long that they don't know anything about the world outside. Chained facing a wall of the cave, they can only see shadows cast by figures passing along the cave's entrance. Finally, one prisoner is freed and led outside. Blinded by the light, he is unsure of the reality before him. Are the figures outside the cave real? Or are the shadows he and his companions had been accustomed to seeing the actual reality? The man pauses, motionless, as he tries to determine what should be his next move.

Listening for God's voice often begins with this type of experience. We may not know right away if it is actually God we are hearing, or other influences and ideas from the world around us. Only in time do we develop the ability to know God's voice and hear it clearly. This becomes easier as our relationship with the Holy deepens and matures. It requires the kind of waiting posture described in the previous chapter: listening quietly for God to speak deep within our hearts.

It is important to remember that our relationship with God is a two-way relationship. We are listening to God, and

God is also listening to us. We listen and God speaks; we cry out to God, and God hears our cry. Our communication with God is a process of speaking and a process of listening, but we must find stillness and quiet, especially as we become newly aware of God's voice.

In the Gospel of John, Jesus says, "I am the good shepherd. I know my own and my own know me" (Jn 10:14). Jesus' comparison of the disciples to sheep is not necessarily flattering—sheep aren't known to be terribly intelligent creatures! Yet, Jesus wants his followers to learn a lesson from the sheep: "...the sheep follow [their shepherd] because they know his voice" (Jn 10:4).

Like the sheep, we don't need to comprehend all at once everything God is saying to us. But, as Jesus tells us, we do need to spend time getting to know God intimately. And the more time we spend in prayer and reflection on the things of God, the more we will come to recognize God's voice.

Practical Tips for Spiritual Listening

Not too long ago, I was watching one of those late-night infomercials. In it, a psychiatrist claimed to have discovered a revolutionary new way to cure high blood pressure. He began to demonstrate his new technique to his viewers. He showed the way one should be seated and how to breathe—a technique which actually comes out of Eastern Mysticism. In some cultures, this might be considered a form of prayer, but this infomercial introduced it as a way to teach people how to control their blood pressure. I laughed and thought to myself, *All those people flocking to this man appear to be Christians, or at least people who have grown up in a Western culture. They just don't know he's teaching them a spiritual technique that has been available in our own Christian tradition for hundreds of years!* In fact, how true it is that many modern spiritual seekers

are unfamiliar with the age-old resources that have been
handed down in their own faith communities.

One ancient form of Christian prayer is known as the
prayer of listening, or the prayer of the heart, which involves
a reflective repetition of a word or phrase. There are those
who, after years of practicing the prayer of repetition, find
that they no longer need it to become centered. However, a
person who is new to this listening process may find this
method helpful to develop the ability to hear God within his
or her own heart.

Those of us who are beginning prayer can draw upon a
wealth of spiritual writers who are both ancient and contemporary. Their writings suggest that time be set aside to
approach God in prayer, and that one should go to the same
place as much as possible. Perhaps a living room or any area
of the house that is quiet will make a good spot for prayerful
listening. I always laugh to think that people today still have
formal and informal living rooms. When I was a child living
in the South, we had a formal living room, the parlor. This
parlor was used only for very special guests or on rare special
occasions. Because as children we were young and messy, we
were not allowed in there. But we also had a family room—
the den—where we usually entertained our family and closest
friends. This was the space where most of our leisure activities happened. As a result, the living room was the place I
used, as a teenager, for prayer and solitude.

Whatever room in your home you may choose, be sure
to sit in a firm but comfortable chair and find a relaxing
position. Then invite God to be present to you, or clearly
state to God that this is a time you have set aside to be
available to God. Select a favorite, simple prayer to repeat
softly. You will probably notice that in repeating the prayer,
your body will begin to slow down and your breathing will
become calmer.

Take notice of your breathing. Inhale and exhale at the same point in your prayer. Although it may seem awkward and mechanical at first, eventually you will find that your body, mind, and spirit will develop a rhythm that is centered in and touched by the presence of God's Spirit. This rhythm acts as a means of opening us or disposing us to the possibility of God's presence being made manifest to us. This is one of the means by which God deepens our relationship with himself.

Take It to the Lord

If you read the psalms you may have noticed how many psalms speak of listening in prayer and telling God our troubles. The psalmist's prayers are often painfully honest about the distress that can sometimes overwhelm us.

> I waited patiently for the Lord;
> he inclined to me and heard my cry.
> He drew me up from the desolate pit...
> and set my feet upon a rock... (Ps 40:1–2).

> Give ear to my prayer, O God;
> do not hide yourself from my supplication.
> Attend to me, and answer me;
> I am troubled in my complaint... (Ps 55:1–2).

Although some teachers of prayer suggest putting aside all our worries when we are praying, others, including myself, advise the opposite. Before beginning a period of prayer, try to remember and name the things that are worrying you. As you begin to think of them, pass them over to the Lord—almost like playing a game of Bridge, when you pass cards over to your partner. If we pass our concerns over to the Lord, the time spent in prayer will provide an opportunity for listening to God's response.

Some people actually like to imagine a container, a lovely container, maybe something sturdy like wood. All of their

problems—illness, addiction, hardship, anger, hurt, etc.—
can be placed in the container, sealed tightly, and passed over
to God. In the Black community, we have these wonderful
African baskets with lids. Some Native American cultures
have "worry baskets," "dream catchers," or similar items.
The basic idea is the same: problems can be imagined con-
cretely, gathered up, and physically contained as if lifted from
one's shoulders.

When we take things to the Lord in prayer, it means telling God of all our troubles and woes. It may seem as if God
does not know our difficulties. However, not only does God
know our troubles; God's compassionate presence is the very
reason why we can even attempt to pray. Thus, it is important to be open and honest as we approach God in our
distress. Rather than waste time turning over in our heads
the various concerns and anxieties we face, we should be
honest with the Lord and lay them down before the One
who carries all of our burdens. This then frees our hearts to
be engaged by God.

There is a favorite nineteenth-century Christian hymn, still
popular today, which reflects well the second movement of
the heart's symphony:

> What a friend we have in Jesus,
> All our sin and grief to bear!
> What a privilege to carry
> Everything to God in prayer.
> O what peace we often forfeit,
> O what needless pain we bear,
> All because we do not carry
> Everything to God in prayer.*

---

*What a Friend We Have in Jesus, Joseph Scriven, 1819–1886.

Listening to God's Healing Voice

When Isaiah received his prophetic call, God's message to him implied that if his audiences truly were to listen to God's words, they would turn to God and be healed (cf. Is 6:10). Such is the case for many spiritual seekers. Prayer, which involves intense listening to God, often results in profound changes and spiritual healing in the heart of the believer. We can become holy in a very real sense, not because of our own actions but because of the activity of God's Spirit within us.

One of my college professors, Father Gilbert Hardy, a Cistercian priest from our Lady of Dallas Monastery, seemed to walk with God all of his life. Many Cistercians had left Hungary during the revolution of 1956; others escaped from the communist state in the early 1960s. While some of the novices were escaping to the free West, they witnessed their classmates being shot down as they fled. Others lost family members. Father Hardy's own father was killed during the war, and he was one of the last of his community to escape, only to return in the mid-1990s and to die in Budapest while attempting to reestablish a seminary there.

One day as I was walking with Father Hardy and discussing an ancient philosophical dilemma, I caught a glimpse of his eyes. I saw so much suffering and pain, and yet a real sense of healing as well. I realized that a lifetime of listening to God, despite the tragic events of his life, had enabled my mentor and spiritual director to develop into a profound thinker and mystic. I recognized in him the quality of holiness, which comes only from listening closely to, and being touched deeply by, God.

People like Father Gilbert, as we called him, allowed God to move deeply within their hearts and to transform their souls. That process of listening in stillness before God allows God to change us from within. It's not the kind of experience in which we look into the mirror one morning and say, "Yes! It's finally working. That magical listening technique is really working! God is transforming me!" Rather, it is a process that makes a difference *within* us, and only over time. The two-way relationship available to us in Christ begins to transform our spirits. We do not forget the pain of the past, but as we hear God's voice we are gradually healed, strengthened, and guided in a process of letting go, so that the problems of the past do not control us. Over the years I have often reflected on how profound it was for me to witness Father Gilbert's healed suffering. And I have attempted during my own times of distress to remember that the Lord heals the brokenhearted (cf. Lk 4:18). But we must be willing to allow God to heal and comfort us.

The need to be open and listen is clearly present in a story from the Gospel of John, chapter 5. There Jesus encounters a man who had been paralyzed for thirty-eight years. Jesus sees the man's suffering and immediately asks him, "Do you want to be made well?" But apparently also paralyzed in heart and mind, the man fails to listen to Jesus. Instead he recites his well-rehearsed excuses for why he is so stuck. So, Jesus commands him to walk—and the man, hearing Jesus' voice loud and clear the second time, is healed!

· · · · · · · · · ·

As believers, we must be inclined toward the voice of God. We must be filled with a desire to allow God to change us, to heal us. This means that we must be willing to listen for the orchestral strains that hearken to the formative stages of God's symphony. And with that we delight in hearing Jesus proclaim:

"Blessed are your eyes, for they see, and your ears, for they hear. Truly I tell you, many prophets and righteous people longed to see what you see, but did not see it, and to hear what you hear, but did not hear it" (Mt 13:16–17).

Chapter Five

The Third Movement
The Struggling Heart:
Dark Nights and Arid Days

"Let nothing disturb you. Let nothing frighten you. All things are passing; God only is changeless. Patience gains all things. Who has God wants nothing. God alone suffices" (*Teresa of Avila*).

The third movement of the heart's symphony differs from that of the musical symphony; the latter is typically upbeat and rhythmic, while the former is solemn and sometimes tumultuous. This third movement refers to the very common experience of spiritual struggle, suffering, or dryness. At some point in the journey, the road gets bumpy; in fact, here the road may seem to have disappeared altogether. The blissful union which some seekers experience in the first two movements ends—suddenly or over time, and sometimes without cause. What does one do when the honeymoon with the Holy seems to be tragically, inexplicably, over?

John of the Cross used the phrase "Dark Night of the Soul" to describe the experience of inner turmoil which results from spiritual distress or stagnation. A contemporary of Teresa of Avila, he spoke of this reality in his spiritual canticle, "The Ascent to Mount Carmel." In the poem, John

57

refers to the dark night as part of the process in which the soul grows in its relationship with God. The challenge of the third movement is that we rarely feel we are growing when we are in the midst of the struggle. Rather, we experience our prayer life as dry or non-existent, and our God as absent or uncaring. We may even feel that God has intentionally and cruelly plunged us into this state of interior suffering. How can such a desolate and dismal interval serve as a prelude to the joyful grand finale of our heart's symphony?

More Than a Fair-Weather God

When I was a teacher in my mid-twenties I had an experience of knowing definitely that I really, *really* did not want to teach certain types of students. I had been out of graduate school for a number of years, and was a pretty good schoolteacher. I wanted to be a better teacher, but I didn't want to work with students who were not the "cream of the crop." One year I was assigned a group of students who literally had the worst grade point averages in the school. I really felt as if I had been messed over: there I was, trying to teach a group of young people who could think of nothing more important than their Friday night date. They had no desire to learn about God or religion; and I had no desire to teach them about anything else.

After several weeks of mutual frustration, one of the students said to me, "You know, if you'd just listen to us, maybe you could figure out how to make us change. If you would listen to us, you'd learn how to teach us." Frankly, I was shocked by this student's candor. I spent some time thinking about those words, and I went back and started listening to my students. At lunch time, I would go to the cafeteria and sit with them, to listen to their stories and find out what was happening in their lives. In the process, I discovered a number of things. First, although my students were academically really not very bright, I certainly shouldn't have put them down. Second, I realized that these young people were actually quite interested in serious questions about life, but not at all interested in data about God, the Church, and religion. What they wanted to know was: How do I live through this day? How do I go home to my alcoholic father who may beat my mother again tonight? How do I go home today, knowing no one will be there, but that soon all of my younger siblings will get home and I'll have to cook their meals and put them to bed, because my parents won't get home from work until the early hours of the morning? What can you do as a religion teacher to show me how to find God in the midst of my life?

I realized that I had been thinking I was going through some kind of spiritual test. However, to use a popular expression, this was not about me. Rather, it was about my students, children who were living through darkness and distress every day of their lives. The reason my teaching them about faith hadn't worked was because I had not learned how to cross over into their life experiences. I had to help them to understand how to deal with the alcoholic parent who came home drunk night after night; or with the fact that, as a kind of surrogate parent, they had to care for their younger siblings; or how to deal with the physical, emotional, or even sexual abuse which they had been experiencing throughout their young lives. I had been so busy looking at my own suffering that I really did not see theirs. But I finally learned that to be a really good teacher, I would need to figure out how to guide my students through very murky waters, to learn that God is real, present, powerful, and caring even when nothing in the course of a day seems to reflect that fact.

Those students taught me one of the most valuable lessons of my life, a lesson which, unfortunately, many adult seekers never learn. Faith is often taught in childish terms: pat answers that are easy to memorize and recite, but ring hollow and prove irrelevant in the face of challenges and tragedies that life eventually brings, even to the most faithful believer. Typically, in order to mature fully in faith, one must pass through a period of suffering and learn to find God when God seems most elusive. We need to learn to recognize God's presence in the stormy nights, just as we learned to recognize it as spiritual children in the sunny days. We do not believe in a fair-weather God, but in the One who guides us even through crisis and pain.

The ancient Israelites, like the students in my class years ago, learned this lesson early in their spiritual journey. Twice, in Exodus 17 and Numbers 20, the story is told of how the Israelites, disillusioned and frightened by their journey in the desert, complained bitterly that God had abandoned them to die of thirst. That place was called Meribah—the place of Contention—because the Israelites responded to their suffering by quarreling.

As believers, we too can become easily disgruntled and disillusioned by the dark nights and arid days of the third movement of the heart's symphony. But we can also learn to respond to adversity in a positive way. One of my high school students had a completely ulcerated stomach, but continued working forty hours a week so that she could pay tuition for herself and her younger sister. One day, she said to me, "My father left us; my mother works, but she can't make much because her health isn't good. I work as much as I can so that we can go to Catholic school and get a good education." I was amazed how that young person was not broken and beaten down by the hardship of her life. She just needed reassurance from time to time that she was not going through all of this because God hated her. Rather, God was strengthening and sustaining her through the struggles of real life. Indeed, I learned a great deal from my students, especially the fact that when we have plunged into the depths of darkness and moved into the desert, we face the greatest challenge: to know and trust God whether we are standing on a mountaintop or in the darkest valley.

The Problem of Innocent Suffering

Many years ago I had the privilege of making a thirty-day retreat. My retreat director assigned me a passage from the book of Job. Throughout his innumerable experiences of loss and distress, Job was silent and steadfast in his faith. But after so much suffering and distress, Job reached his breaking point and began to challenge God, questioning God's love and justice. In response, out of a whirlwind God said to Job, "Where were you when the earth was formed?"

I remember reading those words during my retreat as though for the first time, and I instinctively cringed. I heard God saying to me, "Who are you to question God?" Now I realize there is also another message in that question. God's words to Job were not so much a recrimination for questioning God; rather, they were an affirmation that God indeed has been in control of all things since the beginning of time.

When our lives have gone on smoothly, without a hitch, we tend to think that we have done it all ourselves, that somehow or other we have achieved all of this by our own power and not by God's. When we are suffering, we come face to face with our own weakness and inability to cope. That is when we are forced to depend on God to see us through. But turning to God when one is suffering inno-

cently is not easy. One immediately faces the very common
questions: Why is this happening? Why me? Who is responsible for my suffering?

An awful lot of people think that if God is in control of all
things, then God must be responsible for suffering as well.
In fact, this issue is a matter of continuous debate in the
arena of world theology. However, passing through the dark
night of the soul can give the innocent sufferer new insight
into the power of God. God neither causes evil nor inflicts
suffering; but neither does God necessarily manipulate the
vicissitudes of life to help us avoid pain. Instead, God usually
suffers with us (the root meaning of the word com-passion is
"suffering with") and gives us the strength to survive our
trials.

I often think about a friend's mother who suffers with
arthritis. She cannot move around as well as she used to, and
she frequently says, "Now I really appreciate the times when
I could get up and go!" When she is able to be with others
and is relatively free from pain, she says, "You know, before I
got arthritis, I took a lot for granted. I never appreciated the
freedom of being able to run around doing things."

This woman's experience is very much like that of innocent spiritual suffering. When we go through a crisis or a
time when it seems God is absent, we come into a much
deeper appreciation of the feeling of God's presence. It's not
that suffering is good, and certainly not that it's God's will.
But, as my friend with arthritis often reminds herself, even
pain can be an opportunity for spiritual blessing. Saint Paul
says, "We know that all things work together for good for
those who love God…" (Rom 8:28). Although this thought
does not end our suffering, it can give us hope that something good will come out of it.

If it is difficult to remain faithful in times of obvious suffering and pain, it is perhaps even harder to hold on in times

of spiritual silence or stagnation. It is rare for laity to be taught about those moments when it seems as if God has simply abandoned us. We pray, but there seems to be no answer, no feeling, no passion, no direction from God. Such moments are not necessarily caused by any direct evil or outrageous event. Rather, we simply hit a snag. It seems that something is not quite right, but we cannot figure out what exactly is wrong. At these times, no words seem truer than the psalmist's plea:

> My God, my God, why have you forsaken me?
> Why are you so far from helping me,
> from the words of my groaning?
> O my God, I cry by day, but you do not answer;
> and by night, but find no rest (Ps 22:1–2).

The sense of being abandoned by God, with or without a specific crisis confronting us, can feel like the ultimate experience of desolation. This is like a spiritual "free fall," with no identifiable or explicable cause, and no predictable resolution. The times when God seems silent can feel like an eternity.

During times of innocent suffering—whether caused by the pain of illness, hardship or distress, or from an apparently broken connection with the Holy—we can learn from the psalmist to focus on the good things we have known of God in the past. In lament after lament, the psalmist calls to mind the times when God has indeed been present. And the psalmist, although still in agony, finds strength in the assurance that the same God will not be absent forever.

> Yet it was you who took me from the womb;
> you kept me safe on my mother's breast....
> Do not be far from me, for trouble is near
> and there is no one to help (Ps 22:9, 11).

These things I remember as I pour out my soul:
how I went with the throng,
and led them in procession to the house of God....
Why are you cast down, O my soul,
and why are you disquieted within me?
Hope in God; for I shall again praise him,
my help and my God (Ps 42:4–5).

God Don't Like No Ugly

There was an older Black comedienne years ago named Moms Mabley. As part of her routine she would refer to people who did unkind or otherwise wicked things by using the popular Black folk expression, "Well, you know, God don't like no ugly. Somehow or other God's gonna get you if you do ugly things." The whole idea that God is out to get us and that God has dictated horrible things to happen in our lives is unsettling at best. If the Almighty were truly against us, then indeed we would all be in major trouble! No, quite the contrary; I do not believe God is responsible for evil. Sometimes, as in the case of Job, bad things simply happen without moral cause or explanation.

However, Moms Mabley does remind us that the evil that occurs in our lives can be the direct result of our own sin. Sometimes we make unwise decisions, prefer unloving choices, and pursue unhealthy involvements, which can lead to misfortune and disaster. While God does not cause evil, God may allow us in the third movement to come face to face with the very evil we bring on ourselves.

Various twelve-step programs for people dealing with addiction and co-dependency use the term "hitting bottom" to describe this particular experience of the dark night. A person realizes how far removed he or she is from the way life should be, and that the future will only grow bleaker without a radical change in his or her behavior and attitude. One woman described her experience of hitting bottom in these graphic terms: "I feel as if I'm in the bottom of a huge trash can, and there are banana peels on top of my head and coffee grinds and old egg shells and all kinds of dirt and garbage. That's the way I feel right now. That's the way I feel my soul is right now."

When there is some aspect in our life that needs a radical overhaul, we can feel like we've been cast onto the garbage heap. Sometimes mishaps and misfortunes can be signals to us that change and conversion are needed. Dickens' *A Christmas Carol* reflects this common experience. In that story, Scrooge metaphorically hits bottom when the Ghost of Christmas Future reveals the abysmal outcome of his pitiful life. But unlike Scrooge, we do not have the luxury of a ghostly vision to warn us. Instead, we may actually experience the painful reality of watching our lives fall into apparent ruins. When this happens, the most challenging responses may be required of us: to be vulnerable enough with God, to take responsibility for our actions, and to ask God to help us to change.

Not too long ago I became aware that I was being called to make some changes in my life. Things *had* to change, but I did not *want* to change—at least not on a conscious level. I remember meeting a friend who was the former abbess of her community. During our conversation, she started to laugh and said, "Greer Gordon, I have known you long enough to know when you are not right with the Lord. So, what's going on right now?" I answered, "I don't know, but we are fighting." She asked, "Do you know what you're fighting the Lord about?" "I don't think so," I replied, "but I don't think I want to know, either!" Then she said to me, "That's the problem. When you want to know, you will find out; and when you really want to develop the relationship further, you will change."

I go through an experience like this every now and then—times when I know there is something I am being called to do, yet do not want to do it. And because I don't want to do it, I might even avoid praying for a while. I might avoid going to Mass, or look for all kinds of reasons why I don't have to pray and why I don't have to go and celebrate with other believers. At those times, when I least expect it, I will invariably run into someone who has known me nearly all my life and who can challenge me spiritually. And they do just that, calling me to confront what I am trying to avoid and to be open to God when I most want to hide.

During the dark night, we may not know what it is we are being called to do. Those times can be very humbling. We may claim to want what God wants, to want God to change us, but we are sometimes going to resist change, because we can't see clearly what we are going to be afterward. We don't know where God is leading us.

One thing is certain, however. God is leading us to new life. This may be a painful and even frightening journey, especially when the third movement challenges us to repent and reform our lives. But the words of Moms Mabley, "God don't like no ugly," don't have to threaten us. God is constantly renewing the beauty of all created things.

So Angry I Could Scream

Resistance to change can plunge us into a darkness where it seems nothing can be seen clearly. It seems as if God were not with us at all. Those are the times when we can experience some of the greatest growth in our life of prayer, because, frankly, we find ourselves at war with God. This war is not necessarily expressed with words. People don't usually walk down the street shouting, "No, God! I'm not going to do it!" Rather, the anger usually spills out in more subtle attitudes, posturing, and behaviors. We blame God for our discomfort or misfortune, but since God is not physically in front of us, we choose other targets. We become defensive and perhaps even offensive to those closest to us.

Why do we get angry with God? Sometimes the anger may be a sign that we need to change in a way we may not want to change; or, we may blame God for the disappointments and pain in our life and accuse God of causing us to suffer. If, as Simone Weil suggests, we feel that God has instigated a war of wills with us, our anger may be a defense; we distance ourselves from the One we fear may hurt us.

We may assume that God is testing us, like God tested Abraham in Genesis 22. And we get angry because that test seems so cruel and unfair. How could we possibly prevail against such a strong adversary? How could we win a war of wills against the Almighty? Are we just helpless pawns at God's mercy?

The problem is that we forget so easily that God is on our side. God takes no pleasure in our suffering. On the contrary, many spiritual seekers encounter the compassion of God as they pass through the third movement of the heart's symphony. The dark night becomes the occasion for experiencing, as a lived reality, that God is strength in our weakness. Far from being a threat, God is our defender in times of trouble.

> If it had not been the Lord who was on our side
> —let Israel now say—
> If it had not been the Lord who was on our side,
> when our enemies attacked us,
> then they would have swallowed us up alive,
> when their anger was kindled against us....

Blessed be the Lord
who has not given us as prey to their teeth…
Our help is in the name of the Lord,
who made heaven and earth (Ps 124:1–3, 6, 8).

Another problem is that we often use our anger as a weapon to vindicate ourselves against others, to prove ourselves right, or to get even with someone we feel has taken unfair advantage or hurt us in some way. While anger is a common and understandable response to such situations, it is not always helpful. Circumstances are not always within our control. We can spend enormous amounts of energy being angry and totally powerless to force someone else to change. At those times, it may be helpful to remember some advice from the Letter of James: "You must understand this, my beloved: Let everyone be quick to listen, slow to speak, slow to anger; for your anger does not produce God's righteousness" (Jas 1:19–20).

I had an awful temper as a child. My mother constantly told me, "You really have to pray about your temper." I spent most of my childhood and early adulthood praying to be gentle, praying to be gentle, praying to be gentle—and basically not seeing much in the way of results. As I grew older, there were times when it seemed that I had stalled spiritually, that I was in the depths and would never quite come out. Yet, when I did come through those periods of my life, I somehow had lost some of my tendency to get angry over things that did not really matter. It is very interesting that following the times when I found myself most at the bottom, I discovered I had become more patient.

I no longer have to bear the burden of trying to defend myself against a God who, like a tyrant, is forcing me into some fearful transformation; or against other people who have treated me unjustly. Rather, I find comfort, strength, and release from the necessity of anger in the words of Saint Paul to the Romans—that if God is for us, who can be against us? (cf. Rom 8:31–39)

Recognizing God's Voice in the Turmoil

Of all the biblical figures who teach us lessons about what it means to struggle for spiritual growth, one of my favorites is the prophet Elijah. Elijah was a very faithful servant of God, so faithful, in fact, that he obeyed God's orders to slaughter the prophets of the false god Baal, who were threatening to take control of the religion of Israel (cf. 1 Kgs 18). After carrying out that massacre, Elijah had to flee for his life to escape the retaliation of Queen Jezebel. He found himself in the wilderness, a forty-day journey to Mount Horeb (the same place where Moses met God in the burning bush), where he slept in a cave and awaited God's voice (cf. 1 Kgs 19).

When Elijah told God his terrible predicament, God came to Elijah in a most unexpected way. God was neither in the mighty wind, nor the earthquake, nor the fire which passed by Elijah at the entrance to the cave. But when Elijah hearing "a sound of sheer silence," a quiet voice, Elijah became awestruck, for he recognized the Lord was there in that moment.

The third movement of the heart's symphony can often be similar to Elijah's cave experience. We may indeed be in trouble and greatly in need of God's presence and support. Yet, if we look at the question of the dark night, it may seem as if we cannot hear the voice of God. Our own cries of anguish may be so great that we block out God's response. Or, God may be answering us in a way we fail to recognize. However, as Elijah learned, God does not always split the earth to get our attention. The third movement, therefore, challenges us to still our raging hearts and to trust that God indeed will respond.

Recognizing God's voice—especially in times of crisis or distress—requires an ability to expect the unexpected. The story of Abraham and Sarah (cf. Gen 18) is one good example. Three strangers appeared and informed Abraham that he and his wife, who were both quite on in years and distraught over having no children, were now going to have a son. The scene is referenced in the New Testament as an example of hospitality and love with the striking phrase, "Do not neglect to show hospitality to strangers, for by doing that some have entertained angels without knowing it" (Heb 13:2).

When we experience the dark nights and arid days of our spiritual journey, we may not recognize the opportunities we have to entertain angels, or to be in God's healing presence. During times of suffering, the Lord may send someone who is like an angel. But only if we are ready to expect the unexpected will we recognize the angel as sent by God. There are times when God passes us by, so to speak, but we do not notice. When we are most in the depths we may actually be called most deeply into ourselves to meet God in a new way. We must allow the light of God to transform us so that we can experience God and others anew. This process may take years, but if we trust God, God will strengthen us and help us to weather the storms.

Thy Will Be Done

There is a famous and well-loved Christian hymn which was sung not too long ago at my mother's funeral:

> Precious Lord, take my hand.
> Lead me on, let me stand.
> I am tired, I am weak, I am worn.

Through the storm, through the night
Lead me on to the Light.
Take my hand, Precious Lord,
Lead me home.*

The dark night of the soul can often lead us to a point where we long for release, where we beg for God to guide us to a peaceful place to end our suffering. That experience is shared by Jesus, who prayed in the Garden of Gethsemane, "Father, if you are willing, remove this cup from me…" (Lk 22:42). Yet, despite his deepest anguish and sorrow, Jesus continued, "…not my will but yours be done."

The third movement of the symphony of the heart may be a period in which we reach a deep enough trust in God that we are able to submit our will to God's will, and to trust that God will strengthen us through the crisis. This is a very difficult lesson to learn, but it has a remarkably life-giving outcome. For those times, I often reflect on the words of Saint Teresa of Avila.

. . . .

Let nothing disturb you.
Let nothing frighten you.
All things are passing;
God only is changeless.
Patience gains all things.
Who has God wants nothing.
God alone suffices. Amen.

---

*George N. Allen, 1812–1877; adapted by Thomas A. Dorsey, 1899–1993.

Chapter Six

The Fourth Movement
The Inspiring Summit:
God's Covenant of Love

"In this is love, not that we loved God but that God loved us..." (1 Jn 4:10).

Often, the fourth movement of a musical symphony is the grand finale. It brings to closure all of the themes, rhythms, dissonances, and harmonies of earlier movements in a resounding, dramatic fashion. Likewise, the grand finale of the heart's symphony can bring a great sense of peace and resolution to the spiritual seeker. However, this may or may not be a dramatic spiritual experience. A person may not find answers to all of the questions he or she is struggling with; however, clarity about the individual's life may be achieved in this period. This clarity may shape and guide the person's experiences, attitudes, and perceptions for a lifetime.

The clarity that characterizes the fourth movement is the result of a transformation in our relationship with God. That relationship can be described as a covenant—a sacred and binding agreement between two parties who agree to honor and love each other. To have such a relationship with God is truly transforming, and affects all that we do and how we perceive our world from day to day. As Paul explains, "The

73

love of Christ urges us on.... So if anyone who is in Christ, there is a new creation: everything old has passed away; see, everything has become new!" (2 Cor 5:14, 17)

The musical symphony's finale represents the end of the movement, except for the echoes and resonance remembered. In contrast, in the fourth movement of the heart's symphony, the finale is a continuation and ongoing maturation of an undying relationship. We become acutely aware of the profound impact God has had on our lives, and of how strong is the love that binds us. We learn to consciously recognize the covenant of love to which we have been called.

From Adam to Christ: The Unfolding Love Story

As average, ordinary people it is difficult to fathom a close and nurturing relationship with God that is easily accessible to us. Yet, the concept of covenant reminds us of just that. Not only was there a time when a close and nurturing relationship with the Holy was possible; we still live in such a time. The Scriptures are the faith-records of a believing community's relationship with God. They are the stories of old and new covenants of love between God and humanity. These stories suggest access to a process of spiritual growth, and they can be the basis of a lifetime of prayer and renewal for the average, ordinary believer.

The book of Genesis provides an account of how God created the cosmos and all that is in it (cf. Gen 1), including the first man and woman, Adam and Eve (cf. Gen 2–3). We are told that God gave human beings access to and stewardship over everything in the Garden of Eden. They could name and interact with any animal, and partake of almost any fruit, tree, or bush. God's only restriction was that they not eat of the tree that was located in the center of the Garden (cf. Gen 2:8–9, 15–17). The story implies that humanity delighted in what they had—perhaps without thinking of any other options—and agreed to abide by that one simple rule of life: to abstain from the fruit of the tree in the center. Thus, humanity entered into an agreement, a covenant with God. The Garden was a place of peace and tranquility for Adam and Eve: Eden, the garden of delight where life was bliss and there was no distress in all of God's creation.

Believers are told that after a period of time, the man and the woman decided they would eat the fruit of the forbidden tree. The fact that each of them claimed to have been enticed into the decision by another did not excuse them. Each had made a decision to ignore the agreement they had made with God. Each, independent of the other, decided to break God's rule, and in so doing, broke the covenant with God.

Genesis presents the story of man and woman's betrayal in an interesting way. It could very well be the story of any present day individual caught in an act of defiance or treachery. Adam and Eve attempted to place responsibility for their decision on someone else: the man blamed the woman; the woman blamed the serpent. Neither of them had the integrity to take ownership for the decision each of them had made. Their self-seeking, self-serving motivations proved that at their core there existed a fundamental flaw of character. They were unable to stand in a posture of honesty before God. By partaking of the fruit, they thought they would find equality with God; instead they found themselves distanced from, and fundamentally unable to communicate with, the One with whom they previously had enjoyed an intimate and trust-filled bond.

The intimacy Adam and Eve had shared with God was broken, not because God chose to break it, but because Adam and Eve chose not to live up to their end of the bargain. As a result of the breach, the man and woman were evicted from God's blissful and lush Garden of Eden. They found themselves in a new environment where they had to work very hard for their food and survival. The closeness they once enjoyed with God would now be possible only to the extent that they could relate to God in the harsh realities of that world beyond paradise.

Yet, we are told that God did not allow that valued relationship to end with Adam and Eve's breach of the covenant. Rather, God promised humanity that there would come a time when the relationship would be re-established through a restoration of that original covenant.[*]

As the story of humanity's history unfolds, several characters, the descendants of Adam and Eve, were chosen by God to receive a special covenantal relationship as well. Noah was promised salvation from a devastating global flood. Abraham and Sarah were given descendants who would enjoy the blessing of being God's family forever. Moses received the Torah as God's guidance and instruction in how to live faithfully as God's people. Finally, David, protected and strengthened by God's grace, was given a throne to rule over Israel on God's behalf. Each of these covenants, made not just with individuals but also with whole communities, reflects a feature of ancient Israel's attempt to understand the meaning of being in covenant with the Holy. The lives of these individuals— Noah, Abraham, Moses, and David—typify the struggles of the growing community of faith. God tells them how they should live and how their living in this fashion will bring about a renewal or restoration of that intimate, two-way relationship between humanity and God lost in the Garden.

Christianity celebrates the restoration of the original covenant as the reopening of the gates of heaven through the

---

[*] The language of "restoration of the covenant" is that of Robert C. Neville. His work in the area of covenant theology has greatly influenced my work in this area. Neville's discussion of the restoration of the covenant is largely contained in his *Theology Primer.* 1991. Albany, N.Y.: State University of New York Press.

death and resurrection of Jesus Christ. This restoration brought about the re-establishment of intimacy between God and humanity. In and through Christ's death and resurrection, the previously broken covenant is restored. Humankind is readmitted to a personal relationship with the Holy.

Imagining the Covenant: Metaphors and Analogies

When we say we "hear" God, we mean something altogether different than when we say we hear another person speaking or a television show or a car horn. Because God is intangible, language must be used in the most effective way possible to describe that which, in some ways, is indescribable. Language offers several metaphors that we can use to express the notion of God's covenant of love with us. Five of these—journey, dialogue, family, marriage, and discipleship—are desribed below.

Journey. The Genesis narrative relates how, prior to their treachery, Adam and Eve had walked freely with their Creator through the Garden of Eden. They enjoyed a level of interpersonal contact with God which, even today, most people reserve for their closest and most relaxed relationships. People usually walk only with their close friends, those with whom they can be themselves: relaxed, comfortable, and able to discuss all manner of cares and concerns. Such is the assumption behind the image of the spiritual journey: closeness with God as One who shares each step of our all-too-busy days. Walking with God is a powerful metaphorical expression for an intimate, grace-filled relationship with God. Through the image of the journey with the Holy, we develop an awareness that God loves us enough to be with us in everything we do.

Luke's Gospel account ends with a wonderful journey (cf. Lk 24), which illustrates the power of this image of God's covenant. Following Jesus' crucifixion, two unnamed dis-

ciples leave Jerusalem and are walking toward a town called
Emmaus. They do not know that salvation has indeed occurred through the resurrection of Christ. While they walk,
they are joined by the Risen Lord whom they do not recognize. As Jesus continues to journey with them, he breaks
open for them the meaning of the faith in which they had
grown. Finally, while Jesus shares a sacred meal with them,
they see that it is the Lord.

Walking with the Lord in the fourth movement of the
heart's symphony is like the journey to Emmaus. It is a lifetime of companionship with God, even when we do not
necessarily recognize our walking companion. Furthermore,
to imagine our covenantal relationship with God as a journey
does not mean that there is a prescribed route we must take
to find God. Rather, God is with us all along the way, even in
the midst of our detours and dead-ends. The Trappist monk
Thomas Merton wrote a prayer which expresses beautifully
what it means to journey through God's covenant of love:

> My Lord God,
> I have no idea where I am going.
> I do not see the road ahead of me.
> I cannot know for certain where it will end.
>
> Nor do I really know myself,
> and the fact that I think
> I am following your will
> does not mean that I am actually doing so.
>
> But I believe
> that the desire to love as Christ loved
> does, in fact, please you.
> I hope that I have that desire
> in all that I do.
> I hope that I never do anything
> apart from that desire.

And I know that, if I do this,
you will lead me by the right road,
though I may know nothing about it.

Therefore, will I trust you always,
though I may seem to be lost
and in the shadow of death.
I will not fear,
for I will know you are ever with me,
and you would never leave me
to face my perils alone.*

Dialogue. Another image often associated with God's covenant of love with the believer is that of dialogue. The life of the spiritual seeker can be an experience of an ongoing conversation with the Holy. In the fourth movement, one may become aware that God continually enters one's thoughts. As the psalmist notes,

You know when I sit down and when I rise up;
you discern my thoughts from far away...
Even before a word is on my tongue,
O Lord, you know it completely... (Ps 139:2, 4).

However, this is not just a matter of God hearing our thoughts, our needs, and our petitions. Rather, it means a two-way conversation, which increases our ability to hear God's voice guiding, comforting, challenging, and loving us. Thus, this image of covenantal love involves prayer without ceasing (cf. 1 Thes 5:17).

One example of this prayerful dialogue is reflected in the story about Abraham negotiating with God to forego the planned destruction of the wicked city of Sodom (cf. Gen 18:16–33). A person of compassion, Abraham interceded

---

*Thomas Merton, *Thoughts in Solitude*.

with God on behalf of the people of that city and begged
God not to destroy them. Abraham bargained for the lives
of Sodom's inhabitants, and meanwhile tested God's justice
and compassion as the conversation progressed. God promised Abraham that, for the sake of the righteous Sodomites,
the whole city would be spared. But how was Abraham to
know just how far God was willing to go? Abraham began by
proposing that there may have been as many as fifty righteous people in Sodom; God agreed to clemency for the sake
of the fifty. And what if there were only forty-five, or thirty,
or twenty, or even ten righteous people? Skilled at barter,
Abraham kept lowering the number and raising the stakes;
and each time God promised to be merciful for the sake of
fewer and fewer just people (cf. Gen 18:24–32).

Of course, not even ten just people were found. Thus,
Sodom and the city of Gomorrah were destroyed (cf. Gen
19:24–25). This story does not simply demonstrate how jus-
tified God was in that act of judgment, but it also illustrates
the power of prayerful dialogue with God to reach understanding, insight, and mutual agreement. The covenant of
love involves give and take; it is a two-way relationship between the human being and the Holy.

Saint Teresa of Avila called this prayerful dialogue with a
friend the art of holy conversation. She encouraged the believer to seek and to practice this conversation often. If we
begin to see our covenantal relationship with God as a matter of holy conversation, we may wonder how we can begin
the process of unfolding and opening ourselves fully to God.
And more, how is God made known to us? Matthew says,
"Do not hide your light under a bushel basket" (Mt 5:16).
This image conveys the importance of opening ourselves up
from within. In the fourth movement, we become aware that
the focus of prayer is not on external forms and behaviors,

but on the whispering of God and the groaning of our own spirits deep within us (cf. Rom 8:22–25). We may experience a sense of holy fear and, at the same time, a sense of an all-embracing strength in the realization that God *is* present to us. No one else will hear the conversation that we are experiencing with God. But in this stage of our spiritual life, we clearly recognize that two-way relationship in which we may speak with God, listen to God, and sometimes simply dwell in the silence of God's presence within our hearts.

Prayer is a process for slowing down and walking with the One we say we love. That is why prayer is a metaphor for God's covenant of love. God would not have reopened the lines of communication had God not loved us. Through prayer we rediscover God's invitation to enter the profound love relationship that God established with average, ordinary believers.

Family. One of my favorite people in my life is my father. When I look back on my childhood, I remember my very, very bad temper. My mother would spend a great deal of time telling me how unladylike and sinful it was to lose my temper, but I seemed thoroughly unmoved to conversion. However, periodically, after one of my "episodes," my father would say to me, "Let's go for a walk." And as we walked, he would begin to talk to me a little bit about my behavior. He would start by asking me what had happened and then slowly unfold my part in the deed.

My father's policy with all five of his children was that we were never to let the sun set on our anger (cf. Eph 4:26). So, before the evening ended, no matter what the altercation, no matter what the breach, my father would somehow get me and my siblings to the point where we really had a sense of having to forgive each other—whatever the breach and whoever caused it.

My dad tried to teach all of us how to be in relationship with each other, not just as rivaling siblings, but also as family. Likewise, for many of us, our relationship with God is like a family affair. With God as our Parent (both Father and Mother metaphors are meaningful here), we are challenged and called to learn to live together as covenanted people, even though in so many ways our bonds are broken by sin, pain, and alienation.

Jesus offers a perfect example of this family metaphor for covenant. From his birth and throughout his active ministry, Jesus enjoyed a remarkable two-way relationship with God. There was a give-and-take to such an extent that Jesus referred to God as his Father; and not simply as Father, but as *Abba,* a term young children may use to refer to their daddies.

God's covenant of love in familial terms is reflected powerfully in the First Letter of John:

"See what love the Father has given us, that we should be called children of God; and that is what we are! The reason the world does not know us is that it did not know him. Beloved, we are God's children now; what we will be has not yet been revealed. What we do know is this: when [Jesus] is revealed, we will be like him, for we will see him as he is" (1 Jn 3:1–2).

The fourth movement of the heart's symphony, therefore, offers us an opportunity to experience God and other believers in a unique and challenging way. Like any family, we must learn to love and forgive one another. But we also know that in this family, with God as our loving Parent, we are being continually instructed, transformed, and strengthened to live as God's children even with those who may indeed not know that God loves them as well.

Marriage. Another image for the covenant of love between God and God's people is the image of the marriage relationship. For this point in the spiritual journey, however, the focus is not on the starry-eyed honeymoon lovers, but on the spousal partners who have been through even the dark night of the soul together, and yet have remained faithful and committed.

I come from a time and place where you wouldn't consider a person a suitable candidate for marriage unless you were properly introduced. Of course, there were always some brazen fellows like my eldest brother who came home one evening and announced to my parents, "I saw the girl I'm going to marry." My parents said, "I beg your pardon." He said, "Oh, yes, I saw her across the basketball court." My dad asked seriously, "Son, what do you mean you saw the girl you're going to marry?" And my brother insisted, "Daddy, I saw her. She was sitting right over on the bleachers. I know I'm going to marry that woman." My father, becoming very concerned, said, "Well, Son, have you even met this young woman?" "No," my brother answered, "but I'll make sure I meet her, because someday I'm going to marry her!"

Now, needing to be formally introduced, my brother found a friend who had a friend who knew this young woman. It took three months for him just to arrange to meet her, let alone talk to her. When he finally did, he made certain that there were several other occasions for him to "run into" her. Eventually they dated, and two years later they were married.

The earlier movements of the heart's symphony may offer moments of enthusiasm that seem almost like a romance with God. All is new and exciting and joyful. Then the dark nights and arid days of the spiritual quest can challenge our blissful relationship. That is when the marriage-like covenant of love with God becomes real. God becomes known in the heart of the believer as the One without whom the believer cannot imagine life. Prayerful intimacy with God, and knowledge that one can do nothing apart from God, is similar to a marriage union seasoned with age.

In the musical *Fiddler on the Roof,* one song captures the spirit of this metaphor for God's covenant of love. For the first time, the central characters, Tevye and his wife Golde, come to a realization of the love they have grown into over twenty-five years of married life:

> *Tevye:* Do you love me?
>
> *Golde:* Do I what?
>
> *Tevye:* Do you love me?
>
> *Golde:* Do I love you? …For twenty-five years I've washed your clothes, cooked your meals, cleaned your house, given you children, milked your cow. After twenty-five years, why talk about love right now?…
>
> *Tevye:* Then you love me?
>
> *Golde:* I suppose I do.
>
> *Tevye:* And I suppose I love you, too.
>
> *Both:* It doesn't change a thing, but even so, after twenty-five years, it's nice to know.

Each of us has a unique journey, a special relationship with the Holy. Some of us are aware from the early movements of God's loving presence in our lives. Others of us struggle to come to know that God really does care. The fourth movement, a point of spiritual maturity for the seeker, can be an opportunity to grow into consciousness that the God whom we have sought all along has loved us from the start, and that somehow we have learned to love God, too.

Discipleship. Within the early Christian monastic tradition, it was not at all uncommon for a disciple to walk with the master. This image is consistently practiced within Buddhist, Confucian, and Hindu traditions as well. It is also the prevailing image of Jesus in relationship with his followers. But what is discipleship really? How is this an effective image of God's covenant of love?

Many years ago, I had the opportunity to spend several months in a monastery of contemplative nuns. During that time, my mentor taught me that not all knowledge is gained through the written word or through the process of seated intellectual pursuits. Sister Audrey would take me on long walks around the monastery grounds, during which we would talk about the things of God. The give-and-take of those conversations included my questions and her responses, my responses to her questions, and our shared reflections. We spoke intimately and openly about the ways in which God acts in the life of the one who earnestly seeks God. Those leisurely conversations helped me to learn what it means to walk with the Lord also as my Friend and Mentor. I learned through experience what it means to be a disciple of the Holy.

Few biblical texts offer a more powerful image of discipleship than the Gospel of John, chapters 13–17. In this so-called "Farewell Discourse," Jesus instructs his closest followers in how to continue his ministry; he also reveals to them the transforming quality of the relationship he had established with them during the three years they were together. John 15 is particularly striking: being a disciple means being as closely connected to and dependent upon one's mentor as branches are to the central vine (cf. Jn 15:1–7). Furthermore, living as a disciple in God's covenantal love means that we know the friendship of God (cf. Jn 15:15), a friendship so compelling that we might even lay down our lives for God, as God also lifted up the only Son for the sake of his friends (cf. Jn 3:16).

Discipleship, therefore, is not just learning about God, or even learning how to serve God. Rather, it is being fully transformed by the love of God. Covenant is so much more than an agreement; it is a way of life for those who become inextricably and lovingly bound to their Ultimate Friend.

Covenant and Community

One of the most obvious characteristics distinguishing a musical symphony from a concerto is that the latter features the work of a single instrumentalist, while the former blends a wide range of orchestral players. Likewise, the spiritual journey is not only relevant for individual seekers, but for the community as well. God's symphony is heard in a multitude of hearts, and its beauty lies in the blending and sharing of our varied spiritual experiences and insights. As we look at the covenantal love of God, we need to examine the ways in which that love is nurtured and experienced in the life of the Christian community which we call Church.

It is not possible for us, as individuals or as community, to have a relationship with God unless we have been introduced to God. Within the context of Church, the way we celebrate our initial introduction to God is through baptism. Many people today have moved away from belief in the necessity of baptism. However, when we introduce children or young believers into a relationship with God within the Church, that community becomes the family in which the believer will continue to grow. Baptism, a rite of initiation, celebrates the faith of the Church that the new believer will live with Christ and, upon dying, will also rise with Christ (cf. Rom 6:3–5). At each new baptism, the Church promises to support its new member in living God's covenant of love. The elders of the community must teach the child how to walk with God, to know, believe, and trust in God. That is our responsibility as members of the Church.

The problem is that so many adults do not continue to develop a more mature relationship with God. As children (or new believers) we were introduced to God, but that is not enough. We must deepen our relationship with God through an experience of *mystagogia,* a term the Church uses to describe the process of unfolding and unlocking the mysteries of God. Adult believers support each other in that process through communal prayer, celebration of the Eucharist, and other activities that reflect the work of the Spirit within the life of the Church. Church, then, is where we bring our trust, our faith, our hope, our love, our desire for God, and our care for one another into that communal celebration that enriches us all.

Many of us, however, are afraid to take responsibility for introducing our children into this community. Teenagers especially complain, "Well, what am I supposed to get out of going to church? It's boring!" They think that church is only for the elderly who are afraid they are going to die.

I have a niece who, at fourteen years of age, felt that life was irredeemably miserable. I would often talk with her about why we participate at Mass. She would say to me, "You're either a lunatic or maybe you really are a believer, but I don't get any of this stuff." I discovered that her parents had not taken the time to help her develop her relationship with the Lord. She had been introduced to God through baptism, she had a concept of God, but she did not know God. So I would try to walk with her as my father had with me, and to share with her about how I knew God. I would suggest little ways she could spend quiet time to open herself to the reality of God's presence.

If indeed our churches seem boring, irrelevant or dying, that does not mean that God is any of these things. It is our responsibility as mature believers to share with the community the life and the love with which God inspires us. Our churches will be vivifying and meaningful to the extent that they reflect the power of God's love at work within us. If we do not teach our children about the covenantal love of God, then they are going to miss out on the richness of our life as Church. We will have no communal celebration unless we come together regularly to pray and worship. There is no substance to our belief unless we live out that covenantal relationship, not only with God but with others who seek God as well.

The Death and Resurrection of Christ

Earlier in this chapter, I mentioned the crucial impact which Jesus Christ's death and resurrection had in restoring God's covenant of love with humankind. Because the Lord suffered, died and rose from the dead, the original covenant that God established with the first human beings is somehow restored, repaired, complete. In fact, as Christians, we hear the Easter proclamation, "Today salvation has been wrought! Today God has restored the covenant! Today God has reopened the gates of heaven!" Through the death and resurrection of Christ, God reopens the lines of communication and communion so that we can indeed experience unity with the Holy.

Even before the time of Jesus, men and women talked to God, cried out to God, believed in God, and asked God for salvation and grace. We hear of the prophets, of kings such as David, of the psalmists, sages, and priests, all communicating with God before the time of Jesus. But what the death and resurrection of Christ accomplished was our ability to hear God, both as individual Christians and as Church, in a different way. With the restoration of the covenant, we experience a renewal of our relationship with God, in a way that would be incomplete apart from Christ. Through the blood of Christ, we are restored as children of God and as sisters and brothers to one another (cf. Rom 8:14–17).

Joyful Ode: The Final Chorus

The First Letter of John speaks eloquently of the covenant of love to which God calls us. Even in a world of turmoil and distress, God's love brings us together in fellowship and joy: "We declare to you what we have seen and heard so that you also may have fellowship with us; and truly our fellowship is with the Father and with his Son Jesus Christ. We are writing these things so that our joy may be complete" (1 Jn 1:3–4).

One of the greatest musical symphonies of all time is Beethoven's Ninth. That masterpiece is noted not only for its majestic orchestration, but especially for the innovative way in which the composer ends the work—a choral hymn of adoration and praise:

> Joyful, joyful, we adore thee,
> God of glory, Lord of love!
> Hearts unfold like flowers before thee,
> opening to the sun above.
> Melt the clouds of sin and sadness,
> drive the dark of doubt away.
> Giver of immortal gladness,
> fill us with the light of day!*

To enter into a genuine relationship with God, both as individuals and as community, brings us to the point of overwhelming joy. This covenant of love means that we are truly open to a mutual relationship with God, a two-way conversation, an exciting journey, an unbreakable family bond. The Source of immortal gladness fills us—even through all of our wandering, waiting, suffering, and pleading—with the brilliant light of day.

---

*Lyrics: Henry van Dyke (1852–1933).

. . . .

The "grand finale" of the heart's symphony is far from an ending. Rather, it is the recognition of having arrived at the breathtaking view that uniquely accompanies one's arrival at the Lord's summit. From the summit our walking Companion unfolds for us a more excellent path (cf. 1 Cor 12:31), which serves as the inspiration of our hearts' symphonies. Filled with joy, we affirm with Saint John that "in this is love, not that we have loved God but that {God} loved us..." (1 Jn 4:10). Amen!

Part Three

The Lived Reality

Chapter Seven

Spiritual Harmony:
Balancing Work and Prayer

"For everything there is a season, and a time for every matter under heaven" *(Eccl 3:1).*

In symphonic orchestrations, as in life, the inspired finale is always followed by a return to the original theme. For the believer, that original theme is the everyday reality of life in society, with its marketplace stresses and delights. The Christian's call to be in the world but not of the world (cf. Jn 17:15–16) presents a unique challenge. We are called, as reflected by the French Benedictine Henri Le Saux (a.k.a., Abhishiktananda, in his book, *Prayer)*, to be not only people of prayer, but also to become contemplatives in a world of constant interaction and distraction. The problem is how to be contemplative while attending to all that requires our attention.

For those of us who live in the ordinary work-a-day world, the relationship between work and prayer is a constant challenge to maintain. We are forever attempting to integrate and balance our lives. Somehow or other it seems as if we struggle to pray while we are working, and yet we wonder if we really are able to pray while we are working.

There has been a longstanding debate in the history of the Church. What does it mean to pray and work? Is it better to do our work first and later to pray? Or can we pray while we work? The Benedictines have a motto: "Ora et labora," prayer and work. Friends of mine who are Benedictine nuns joke about this phrase, saying, "Ora et labora, et labora, et labora, et labora...." Life in a Benedictine monastery, however, attempts to find a balance, to blend work and prayer in the life of the Christian believer.

Mary and Martha: Two Sides of One Coin

During the Middle Ages, one of the spiritual descendants of Saint Benedict was Saint Bernard of Clairveaux, who wrote a lengthy treatise about the two sisters, Martha and Mary (cf. Lk 10:38–42). Luke tells us that Mary remained seated at the feet of the Lord, listening as he taught in her home. Meanwhile, Martha was anxious and harried as she prepared the meal for their honored guest. Trying to be an attentive hostess, and aware of the needs of all those around her, Martha was busy about many things. These two sisters, the Do-er and the Non-Doer, could represent different ways in which believers may seek the Lord: some through activity, others primarily through contemplation. In addition, the difference between the two reflects the struggle within as each of us tries to find a balance between our work and our life of prayer.

During the Medieval Period, there were many discussions about the relationship between contemplation and service. These discussions centered on the question of who was more present to God: Mary in her listening to Jesus, or Martha in her preparing and serving Jesus? That debate continued, even though Jesus' admonishing words to Martha in the Gospel are clear: "Mary has chosen the better part" (Lk 10:32).

Yet, I don't think Jesus really meant that, in choosing contemplation, one should avoid service to others. Somehow, all of us have to engage in prayer, both when we are active and when we are still. The problem for us as laity (and, in fact, for anyone engaged in ministry or work in the Church) is learning how to blend the two. How is our work prayer? And how does our prayer become work? These are certainly difficult questions. How can we be present to other people and, at the same time, be present to the Lord? What does it mean to find the "balance"?

Two Contemporary Role Models

The twentieth-century Church was blessed with two remarkable individuals who achieved such a balance: Dorothy Day, founder of the Catholic Worker Movement, and Thomas Merton, a Trappist monk at Gethsemane Abbey. These two ordinary people lived extraordinary lives and left a tremendous legacy for future generations.

Through the Catholic Worker Movement, Dorothy Day taught Christians how to identify with and respond to the needs of the poor, the homeless and hopeless, those who scuffled, who labored, who were broken. In fact, many who had been homeless and needy followed in her footsteps by founding other Catholic Worker houses in cities across the country.

Interestingly, Dorothy Day's life truly reflected a balance of work and prayer. On the one hand, she was like Martha, ever serving the needs of the community, of the Church, of others. She reflects that model of the Church which Cardinal Avery Dulles calls the "servant model," reaching out to others in need and thereby following the Gospel mandate that whatever we do to the least among us, we in fact do to Christ (Mt 25:40).

Yet, at the same time, Dorothy Day was a woman of deep reflection and profound insight. She knew the Lord personally as someone dear and necessary to her soul. We see in Day a person who first developed a relationship with the Lord, who then called her to do something, to take action. Motivated by an intense life of prayer, she found herself led to serve the needs of the poor, assisting those who had no one else even to notice them. And through that experience of service, Day found herself compelled to embrace an even deeper life of reflection and prayer.

Dorothy Day was a woman whose inner life with God radiated outward, touching the lives of all around her, of people who may never before have known or been touched by God. She did not merely listen to or preach the words of Christ; she lived them.

Thomas Merton is another example of an individual who deeply sought God. His autobiography, *The Seven Storey Mountain,* tells of his conversion to Christ and eventual entrance into the monastery at Gethsemane, in Kentucky. Named after the garden where Jesus prayed on the night he was betrayed, Gethsemane Abbey is known for its rigorous and ascetical way of life, spiritually very challenging. In the monastery, Merton developed an intense life steeped in God and detached from the plenty of the world. Rooted in the Benedictine tradition, Trappists also adopt an ethic of balancing work and prayer. As one works, one prays. The work of the Trappist involves manual labor, requiring less conscious thought and thus freeing one's mind easily to engage God. However, as Merton learned, the only way that this intense, inner connection with God can occur while one is working is if it happens at other times as well. Merton teaches us to set aside time for silent prayer, which will sustain us even in the noise and busyness of our everyday lives.

Saint Paul calls all who are in Christ to a life of unceasing prayer (cf. 1 Thes 5:17). As laity working in the modern world, we may find it difficult to develop the ability to pray without ceasing. How can we be present to God and at the same time be present to others? Thomas Merton and Dorothy Day serve as modern examples of how to strike the balance, integrating and harmonizing the gifts of both Mary and Martha. They show us that, as Church, we must minister to those who are suffering, not only monetarily, but psychologically, socially and spiritually as well. Whenever we are available to people in this fashion, we are, in fact, allowing the love of Christ to radiate outward from within us. We become transformed in our prayerful work and active prayer.

Holidays and Holy Days

Several years ago, I spent a year in a Benedictine monastery of women. I needed some time away for intense prayer. It was the first time I really understood what Paul meant by "unceasing prayer."

I noted that, in mopping floors, cooking meals (for a hundred folks!), and other chores, activity became so automatic that it was possible simultaneously to engage in thoughtful reflection and conversation with God. This experience led me to think about mothers who prepare large holiday meals at times such as Thanksgiving, Christmas, and Easter. It is so easy to get swept up completely in the doing. We get caught up in the hurriedness and hassle of the holiday festivities. And, like so many New Year's resolutions, we insist each time that we will not fall into the same trap again, only to produce an even bigger flurry of activity when the next holiday arrives.

The holiest days can be simple family times, when everyone pitches in and gathers at table to share a meal and conversation. If we avoid frenetic and frenzied activity, we can keep our holidays holy; the Lord's Day can truly be a day of rest; and the work of preparing the meals and celebrations can bring us closer to God and one another, rather than leave us exhausted and filled with distress.

I have a policy now: whenever I prepare a large meal, I refuse to allow myself to become irritated or upset if something burns or doesn't turn out as I had planned. Setting a slower pace for hospitality preparations can, indeed, be a loving act, allowing one to be more present to those gathered and to God. Mary and Martha may both be needed to help get food on the table, but they also both need to make time to relax and engage the Holy.

Ordinary Time and Extraordinary Time

The time I spent in the monastery taught me how to carry my prayer into the ordinary stuff of my life. How do we do that when we are working in busy, public places? How can we stay prayerful in an office, a traffic jam, a store, a hospital, a manufacturing plant where we find ourselves working every day? How do we allow ourselves to stay in touch with the Lord in ordinary time?

I think the way to do this is by pausing briefly throughout the day to take a spiritual "time-out." We have to remind ourselves consciously that we are in relationship with God. Although our ordinary work may not have anything to do directly with a life of prayer or service, we can still ask God to be present to us and help us be present to God. If we do this periodically throughout the day, then praying will become as automatic as our breathing; and God's transforming presence will turn our ordinary days into extraordinary ones of new insights and profound peace.

Unceasing prayer does not have to be a question of praying the Hail Mary or the Our Father over and over. One does not have to memorize a Scripture passage. It does not even have to mean talking to God. Rather, I am referring to a posture, a way of standing before and walking with God, of being in God's presence. Like Mary, we need to stand in the gaze of God and to keep ourselves mindful of that stance.

Many years ago, I had a spiritual director named Sister Fidelis, a Poor Clare contemplative nun in New Orleans, Louisiana. I was a young person trying to develop a life of prayer and trying to figure out what it meant to be a good religion teacher. I wanted to maintain a close relationship with the Lord, but at the same time I needed to be present to my students. One day Sister Fidelis asked me to reflect on one very brief phrase: "Enoch walked with God" (Gen 5:24). She said, "You know, Greer Gordon, to walk with God means that, somehow or other, you are standing within the gaze of God, in relationship with God."

Her words rang with awesome simplicity. When we walk with God, as Enoch did, it not only means that God is by our side. It also means we are being guided always toward deeper intimacy with the Holy. If we live within the gaze of God, then even when we get caught up in our work, our family life, and the many demands on our time and attention, our relationship with God will continue to deepen. Frankly, God will never let us stray too far. That posture makes all the difference in our quality of life, because each day of ordinary time brings us a step closer to the extraordinary reality of union with our God.

A Lifetime in Balance

To work and pray at the same time presupposes at the outset that we are people of prayer. For years I was a cigarette smoker; like many, I was constantly trying to quit. Then, one day my physician gave me some invaluable advice: "Think of yourself constantly as a non-smoker. If you have a cigarette, think of it as a slippage; basically, you are a non-smoker who on occasion slips and has a cigarette." And I had many years of slips!

What my doctor was suggesting was a change in my attitude and self-image. And in the years since I have quit smoking, I've thought about how that kind of change is relevant to so many areas of our lives. We laity in the modern workplace are not usually trained to think of ourselves as people of prayer. We have not developed a prayerful posture in our daily lives, because we do not yet have those intense periods when we can engage deeply in contemplative prayer. We need to learn how to think of ourselves as people of prayer. Even as we are working we should become like Dorothy Day and Thomas Merton, so rooted in prayer that our relationship with God radiates through all we do. Our communication with God becomes one with who we are, part of our very identity. Without uttering a word, we become believers aware of the loving presence of God, believers who bring that presence into an unsuspecting marketplace.

. . . .

Finally, we must become mindful of the content that fills our periods of thought and contemplation. We need to read, reflect, and take the time to internalize the core of the Christian life. If we read Scripture regularly, participate in the eucharistic liturgy or other Christian worship, and periodically share with others our insights about and experiences with the Lord, then our prayer and work will become less compartmentalized and more integrated within us. All of these things nurture our relationship with God. If we truly love God, and, as the psalmist says, if we long for God as a deer longs for running streams, prayer will become a lifelong venture we gladly embrace. Amen.

Chapter Eight
Spiritual Peace: Walking Justly and Acting Rightly

"Let justice roll down like waters,
and righteousness like an
everflowing stream" (Amos 5:24).

Pope Paul VI is frequently quoted as saying, "If you want peace, work for justice." In fact, prophets like Amos and Jeremiah from the biblical world, and Mahatma Gandhi and Martin Luther King, Jr. from the modern world, remind us that there can be no peace in a world without justice. Indeed, the harmonies of God's symphony in our hearts find their fullest expression as we learn to walk justly and act rightly, even in our daily lives.

What does it mean to live in a posture of justice? Christians are expected to live a life that is just and righteous. The Church's social teachings consistently call us to witness to Jesus' preference for the poor and the oppressed, those who suffer and mourn, and those who are vulnerable in any way (Mt 25:31–46).

To adopt spiritual peace as a life stance means we allow our lives to be so utterly transformed by prayer that we can no longer ignore the plight and concerns of the world around us. It also means that we can no longer conduct "business as usual." We must face the fact that we have a moral responsibility to evaluate the consequences of our actions, to ensure that all that we do results in justice for others, regardless of whether or not they are believers in Jesus Christ. To put it simply, we are indeed our sisters' and brothers' keeper; and this is not a particularly popular concept in our society today.

What are justice and righteousness? Both terms are used in the legal field, but they have slightly different connotations. Justice refers to fairness and satisfaction with regard to the demands of the law. The expression "justice is blind" refers to impartiality in the law's application: a blindfolded "Lady Justice" holds the scales and is not swayed by extenuating circumstances or extraneous considerations which might tip the balance of judgment.

Righteousness, however, is not blind. It not only sees evidence on the surface but probes beneath to allow for as broad and as deep an evaluation of the circumstances as possible. Righteousness is justice tempered by compassion; righteousness is what motivates people to "do the right thing," even when a response is not legally required.

To give an example, if I acquire a million dollars by legal means, justice says I am free to do with the money as I please. Righteousness, however, forces me to ask the question: is it fair that I should keep all of this when with it I could help alleviate suffering? To further complicate the illustration, what if I acquire a million dollars in a way that, although perfectly legal, results in the suffering and oppression of others? Then my moral responsibility is even greater, not only to share what I have, but to work as hard as I can to address that situation of suffering from which I have benefited, even if such action means giving up my privilege.

Both justice and righteousness are necessary to maintain a stable society. Without justice, there would be no consistent code of behavior, social structure, or means to rectify wrongdoing. But without righteousness, a society would run the risk of condoning and perpetuating a world that is heartless and cruel. If everyone were to believe they had no moral responsibility to anyone but themselves, then the Gospel message would be rendered empty and meaningless.

As believers we find ourselves living in a world that often does not seem to know who we are and what we are about. We try to live as Jesus taught us, but at the same time we have to be realistic about the fact that much of our lives may be governed by forces that challenge those Christian teachings. Saint John reminds us that we are called to live in the world but not to be of the world; we must always be aware of those around us, but not controlled by values that are not of God (cf. Jn 17:14–15). How can we, as average, ordinary believers, be true to ourselves, to our God, and to our calling in a world that in so many ways does not know God?

Reverence for God and the Image of God

Of all the Ten Commandments, I think the one which modern Western believers think least about is: "You shall not make for yourself any graven image." Sophisticated people today do not go around making statues representing gods. However, there is much more to this commandment than pagan idols (cf. Ex 20:4). The ancient Israelites not only had to struggle to proclaim their faith in one God amidst nations that worshiped many competing deities; they also insisted that there was only one true image of God, and that the Creator alone could fashion it:

> So God created humankind in his image,
> in the image of God he created them;
> male and female he created them (Gen 1:27).

At the most basic level, acting justly and living rightly means that in our dealings with people we recognize and

rence each and every human being as a person made in
God's image. We must reverence the fact that all people are
children of God and possess a dignity that demands our ut-
most respect. If we understand this fully, we will see other
individuals not as objects to help us achieve our goals, but as
neighbors and siblings whom Christ calls us to serve in a
global community. Justice and righteousness begin with fundamental respect for others, and this means recognizing the
dignity of all human persons.

Conversion through Prayer

To see and reverence all people as reflections of God or as
God's children is easier said than done. It requires an inner
spiritual conversion achieved only through prayer and the
work of God's Spirit within us. Yet, that conversion process
is the key ingredient in reconciling our values with our actions—what we say we believe and how we live our lives.

In my youth during the 1960s, I had several friends who
left college and entered military service. One of them re-
turned from Vietnam a broken man. He could not seem to
get his life together, even though the woman he loved was
trying to be as supportive as possible. After some time had
passed, they broke off their wedding plans and seemed to go
in separate directions. Eventually, however, he sought counseling, began working through some of his issues and,
despite the continued distress in his life, was reconciled with
his fiancée, whom he later married.

Several years later on a return visit home, I ran into my
friend unexpectedly at Mass. He greeted me joyfully and
said, "I finally got my act together. I've had the same job for
five years. Jane and I are expecting our first child, and things
are really working out." As I joined the couple later that day

in their home, I learned more about how this dramatic turn of events had occurred. My friend had spent years in therapy to deal with his traumatic experiences in Vietnam. But the real change happened when he met a priest who had been in the military during the Second World War. My friend said, "He knew the tragedy, the sorrow of war. And that priest walked with me for two years, talking about the most distressing things and asking me how I was going to take that experience and make it life-giving in the here-and-now!"

As a result of the prayerful support of this priest, not only was my friend able to keep a job and maintain a healthy married life; he also became involved in working with children at risk. He began volunteering several hours a week with children who had been abandoned and abused. He had taken the pain of his experience of war and, through prayer, transformed it into service for peace. The conversion within his own life has radiated outward to touch the lives of others. He is righteous and compassionate; and as a children's advocate, he now works for justice.

My friend's desire for God has radically transformed him. He has been led by the Lord to live differently, to care for others, to reflect the justice and compassion of God in a world of violence, neglect, and abuse. Those of us who claim to be in a covenant relationship with God must become sensitive to those who are suffering around us. Conversion compels us to reach out and connect with all who are in need. Whether through service to children, the elderly, the poor or the infirm, the message of Matthew 25 is clear: however we treat the most vulnerable and dejected in our society is how we treat God. And our acts of righteousness rooted in spiritual conversion—or lack of such—will provide the basis for God's judgment of our lives.

Picket Fences and Good Neighbors

I have heard of situations in which neighbors all but terrorize each other. They may go to the same church, shop in the same stores, even work at the same location. But by losing perspective regarding some trivial or not-so-trivial offense, neighbors can begin treating each other like archenemies, disrupting any semblance of peace in a neighborhood.

Conversion should lead us to a greater desire to connect with others, not to a greater resolve to build higher, stronger fences. My friends who live in monasteries understand this. As one told me recently, "I was never so in touch with the world as I have been in this monastery." We often think people in monasteries are isolated. Yet, it is amazing how closely they embrace the problems of the world. And those within monastery walls live in very close proximity to each other. They know well the importance of being good neighbors.

Acting justly and walking rightly means that we need to be good neighbors in the world. Literally, the greatest acts of kindness can be simply sharing a meal, running an errand, or making a quick phone call to a neighbor who is sick, infirm, or lonely. If a neighbor seems intent on offending us, we have an obligation to do all we can to defuse the situation: both by ensuring our basic security (involving law enforcement, if necessary) and by resisting the temptation to escalate the animosity through our retaliation. There can be no peace without justice and righteousness; if our neighbor doesn't know that or doesn't care, then we must do our best to set things right.

Family Feud

Two common proverbs reflect a dilemma in many family relationships. The first is, "charity begins at home." Logic dictates that we should be fair and just at least with our family members. However, human nature invariably leads us to withhold justice and compassion from the very people who are closest to us. Why? Because "familiarity breeds contempt."

Two friends of mine, a mother and daughter, were very close when the daughter was a child. Now the daughter is grown and has become a mother with young children of her own. Well, this daughter quickly developed the habit of dropping the children off at Grandma's unannounced, while she ran errands or kept appointments. Naturally, the grandmother loves her daughter and grandchildren, but she resents being treated like a ready-made babysitter. The daughter, on the other hand, feels resentful that her mother is not willing to support her need for impromptu childcare. The inability to hear one another has clouded over their ability to see each other's need for care.

Often significant family feuds begin with situations not much more serious than this. If both women paused long enough to remember that each is made in God's image, and that each could be enriched if she would be more sensitive to the dignity and needs of the other, then a compromise might enable the two to reestablish the close relationship they once enjoyed.

Of course, not all family conflicts are as clearly defined or as easily resolved. Some feuds were started so long ago that the conflict continues only because family members have grown accustomed to not getting along with each other. Other family feuds reflect complex factors requiring outside intervention through counseling and even mediation. For many of us, however, acting justly and walking rightly can mean simply reordering our priorities so that we respect those closest to us as children of God, despite the flaws that we can see so clearly because we are so close. If we act justly and compassionately with those closest to us, we will begin to make a difference in the lives of all around us.

The Great Misnomer: Charity as an Option, Not a Duty

It is amazing to me when I walk around the City of Boston, or Washington, or any other city in America, that multitudes of people are without homes. These are human beings, someone's child, someone's father, someone's mother, someone's sibling. Yet, most people ignore the homeless as if they were no longer human; in fact, it is as if they were invisible. Often we are in such a hurry that we fail to notice there are people around us in need. We may even justify our indifference by convincing ourselves that people are homeless because they want to be; or because they were irresponsible and got what they deserved; or because there is a breakdown in the system, which is someone else's responsibility to address.

The Roman Catholic Bishops of the United States wrote a pastoral letter on the economy in 1986, when I was working on staff in the Archdiocese of Washington, D.C. A tremendous uproar ensued from various segments of the American Catholic population over what the Bishops said about money and the economy. The problem is that most people, good and just Christian believers, do not understand that how we use our money and where we decide to spend and invest it say an awful lot about how we function as a just society. We believers live not only within the Church, but also within secular contexts that may function by values indifferent to, or even in conflict with, Gospel mandates.

One example is the use of tax revenue for purposes that may not sufficiently provide for the material needs of all people. The Bishops' pastoral letter offered reflections on how political and economic policies can force people into poverty. The letter provided an opportunity for dialogue and assessment of the far-ranging implications of those policies in the context of social justice. However, the Bishops were met with resistance from Catholic laity, who insisted that the Church should address spiritual matters and leave the economy to market forces.

How can we claim to be a people of peace if we do not maintain a strong commitment to justice for all? How can we claim to have experienced any genuine spiritual conversion if we remain indifferent to those in need? It is not enough to care for those in our immediate proximity; we live in a global community, share in a global economy, and the people of other nations are as affected by our economic values and behaviors as those with whom we stand in line at the local grocery store.

The First Letter of John warns that "those who say, 'I love God,' and hate their brothers or sisters, are liars; for those who do not love a brother or sister whom they have seen, cannot love God whom they have not seen" (1 Jn 4:20). Christian love is not just spiritualized sentiment; rather, it is faith transformed into action. As the Letter of James insists, if we turn our backs on one among us in need, our faith is dead (cf. Jas 2:15–17). If we resist the prophetic voices of the Bishops regarding our economic policies and practices, perhaps the story of the rich man and Lazarus (cf. Lk 16:19–31) will remind us that God's standard of justice and righteousness stands in conflict with that of the world.

Racism and Xenophobia

If we are really committed to acting justly, that commitment must be reflected in every aspect of our lives. We have to treat each person with dignity, with respect rooted in our belief that all people are made in God's image. Our prayer life should be the source from which flows our ability to honor all people in a fundamental way, even individuals who may seem different from those with whom we personally identify.

Yet, there is a tragic level of competition, animosity and violence between various groups of individuals in our society today. People of color who have benefited from "Affirmative Action" programs in the past are resented by some who claim that such programs give an unfair advantage to unworthy recipients. Our neighborhoods, schools, and workplaces are filled with those who refuse to respect others who reflect a racial, cultural, or religious heritage different from their own. People can become quickly polarized, judging or even condemning one another for differing ideological or moral values. Anti-Semitism is quietly and surely on the rise, with vandalism and desecration of sacred spaces dismissed as mischievous acts committed by wayward youth. Immigration policies become less hospitable and more foreboding, in a nation comprised almost entirely of the children of immigrants. And, in the wake of hate crimes targeting gays and abortion rights advocates, all too many good Christians remain silently indifferent or self-righteously smug.

Where I travel I frequently see a poster with a certain quote. It poses a powerful question, one I am not sure the average, ordinary believer often takes to heart. The reflection comes from Pastor Niemoeller, a Christian who was incarcerated by the Nazis during World War II.

> First, they came for the Jews
> and I did not speak out
> because I was not a Jew.
>
> Then they came for the communists
> and I did not speak out
> because I was not a communist.

Then they came for the trade unionists
and I did not speak out
because I was not a trade unionist.

Then they came for me
and there was no one left
to speak out for me.

When will it end? When will we learn that the commandment to love one's neighbor is not limited to people with whom we share visible and comfortable common bonds? If we are satisfied to omit any group of people from our commitment to justice and righteousness, we have not yet caught on to what it means to live in a just society under God. As people of prayer, we must embrace, on a global scale, the cause of those who seem most different from ourselves. This is one means by which the believer assists God in bringing the light of Christ into a world of darkness.

Too often we hold back. Sometimes we assume that we should not invade anyone else's life. *Mind your own business. Fend for yourself. To each his or her own.* In addition, in our society many of us are so afraid of someone else getting the upper hand that we resist being risk-takers for peace. We are afraid we are going to get hurt. We are afraid we are going to be sued. We are afraid the cost of compassion will be too high.

The fact of the matter is that the cost of discipleship is high. The Good Samaritan took time out of his schedule and money out of his pocket to help a stranger in need (cf. Lk 10:29–37). If we claim to be following the Lord, we have to let God transform us in such a way that we can cross over into the experience of those in need and work for change.

Justice, Righteousness and the Quest for Peace

As people of faith, we must be aware of everything around us and commit ourselves to bring both justice and righteousness, with compassion, to all. That is what it means to share in the suffering, death and resurrection of Christ Jesus. If we claim to be in relationship with God, we will be sensitive to and aware of our dependence on others. If we are people who act justly, we will be risk-takers committed to working for justice for the most vulnerable and rejected among us. If we are truly righteous, we will be willing to go the extra mile, to do the right thing for the good of another, even when no sacrifice on our part is required.

Saint Francis of Assisi prayed:

> Lord, make me an instrument of your peace.
> Where there is hatred, let me sow love.
> Where there is injury, pardon.
> Where there is doubt, faith…
>
> for it is in giving that we receive.
> It is in pardoning that we are pardoned.
> It is in dying that we are born to eternal life.

. . . .

If we want peace, we must work for justice.
And if we wish to resonate fully with God's symphony
of the heart, we must embrace the call to righteousness
for all of God's people. If the Spirit is truly alive
within us, then our journey is well underway! Amen.

auline
BOOKS & MEDIA

The Daughters of St. Paul operate book and media centers at the following addresses. Visit, call or write the one nearest you today, or find us on the World Wide Web, www.pauline.org

California
3908 Sepulveda Blvd., Culver City, CA 90230; 310-397-8676
5945 Balboa Ave., San Diego, CA 92111; 858-565-9181
46 Geary Street, San Francisco, CA 94108; 415-781-5180

Florida
145 S.W. 107th Ave., Miami, FL 33174; 305-559-6715

Hawaii
1143 Bishop Street, Honolulu, HI 96813; 808-521-2731
Neighbor Islands call: 800-259-8463

Illinois
172 North Michigan Ave., Chicago, IL 60601; 312-346-4228

Louisiana
4403 Veterans Memorial Blvd., Metairie, LA 70006; 504-887-7631

Massachusetts
Rte. 1, 885 Providence Hwy., Dedham, MA 02026; 781-326-5385

Missouri
9804 Watson Rd., St. Louis, MO 63126; 314-965-3512

New Jersey
561 U.S. Route 1, Wick Plaza, Edison, NJ 08817; 732-572-1200

New York
150 East 52nd Street, New York, NY 10022; 212-754-1110
78 Fort Place, Staten Island, NY 10301; 718-447-5071

Ohio
2105 Ontario Street, Cleveland, OH 44115; 216-621-9427

Pennsylvania
9171-A Roosevelt Blvd., Philadelphia, PA 19114; 215-676-9494

South Carolina
243 King Street, Charleston, SC 29401; 843-577-0175

Tennessee
4811 Poplar Ave., Memphis, TN 38117; 901-761-2987

Texas
114 Main Plaza, San Antonio, TX 78205; 210-224-8101

Virginia
1025 King Street, Alexandria, VA 22314; 703-549-3806

Canada
3022 Dufferin Street, Toronto, Ontario, Canada M6B 3T5; 416-781-9131
1155 Yonge Street, Toronto, Ontario, Canada M4T 1W2; 416-934-3440

¡También somos su fuente para libros, videos y música en español!